History of Denmark

A Captivating Guide to Danish History

Free Bonus from Captivating History (Available for a Limited time)

Hi History Lovers!

Now you have a chance to join our exclusive history list so you can get your first history ebook for free as well as discounts and a potential to get more history books for free! Simply visit the link below to join.

Captivatinghistory.com/ebook

Also, make sure to follow us on Facebook, Twitter and Youtube by searching for Captivating History.

Contents

Introduction

At the turn of the 16th and 17th centuries, British playwright William Shakespeare wrote his famous play *The Tragedy of Hamlet, Prince of Denmark*. In Shakespeare's work, the heir to the Danish throne struggles to keep his inheritance as the future king of Denmark, along with his sanity and will to live. The most famous part of the play is Hamlet's soliloquy, which begins with the famous words "To be or not to be" as Hamlet speaks his thoughts on life, its turmoil, and his contemplation of suicide.

Hamlet does not have a happy life. The twists, turns, and the setting of the play (Elsinore Castle, which is the English name for the real Kronborg Castle on the eastern Danish coast) have led non-Danish people throughout the world to believe the Danes and their Scandinavian brethren from Norway and Sweden are a brooding, taciturn lot.

In actuality, over the past twenty years, the Scandinavians have been consistently considered some of the happiest and most satisfied people on the face of the earth. At the end of this book, you will find a link to the United Nations-sponsored World Happiness Report, which has named Denmark the happiest country in the world a number of times. It has been in the top five or ten since the report began in 2011.

The report reflects data on life expectancy, health, income, literacy/education, peace/war, social security, incarceration rates, and more. Over the past four years, Finland (another Scandinavian country) has claimed the number one spot, but in 2021, Denmark was once again in the top five, coming in at number two.

We will talk more about what exactly makes the Danes so "happy" toward the end of this book. Much of this book will be spent telling you about the long and sometimes very painful and warlike history of the oldest kingdom in Europe.

Chapter 1 – Before the Vikings

Illustration 1: Modern Denmark. "Kattegat" from the TV series Vikings is not a town but a waterway/bay.
https://commons.wikimedia.org/wiki/File:Elling_on_denmark_map.jpg

Denmark is a small but strategically placed country. For centuries, the control of Denmark meant not only power and influence but also incredible riches due to its access to the North and Baltic Seas. The kingdoms most affected by Denmark's control of the access into and out of the Atlantic were Sweden and Russia, although every nation east of Denmark on the Baltic Sea was affected by that control.

Of the nations that lay east of Denmark on the Baltic coast, only Sweden and Russia posed a true naval threat, but that was not until the 1500s for Sweden and the late 1600s for Russia. To the west, German coastal cities and what became the Netherlands (also referred to as Holland) eventually caused naval economic competition, but this did not really affect the Danes until the 14th century when the Germans formed the famed Hanseatic League. The Netherlands would become more of a competitor beginning in the 17th century.

Of course, centuries before the Bronze Age, which began in central Europe in about 1900 BCE, the peoples of Europe were relatively isolated and lacked the ability to create true sea-going ships. Therefore, most of the raiding and trading in Denmark was done along the Danish coastline and that of modern Germany and Sweden. When we speak of "raiding" before the Late Nordic Bronze Age (the development of bronze technology came to Scandinavia about a hundred years after Central Europe), we're talking about small and sporadic tribal raids. These were not the famous raids that happened a few hundred years later during the Viking Age.

As time went by, local, regional, and national rulers built fortresses and coastal defenses to protect themselves and control seaborne traffic traveling through the straits on Denmark's eastern coasts. This did not happen in earnest until the Late Nordic Bronze Age (c. 1700–500 BCE).

The Stone Age People

Denmark has been peopled since the Late Stone Age, after the ice sheet that covered most of central and northern Europe receded some eleven to twelve thousand years ago. A series of primitive cultures lived in the area of Denmark, beginning with the hunter-gatherer cultures known as Ahrensburg (named for significant archaeological discoveries near the town of Ahrensburg, north of Hamburg, Germany) and Swiderian (for the Swider River in modern Poland). Both the Ahrensburg and Swiderian cultures were nomadic or at least semi-nomadic. They had no real permanent settlements in the area around Denmark, and it is possible they did not interact with each other.

The semi-nomadic Maglemosian culture was the first permanent culture in Denmark (including the area of today's northern Germany on/near the Danish peninsula known as Jutland). In Danish, *magle mose* means "big bog." Many finds from this culture (8000–6000 BCE) have been well-preserved by the cold, wet bogs found in the area. Scholars have found the remains of huts and the body of the "Koelbjerg Man," which was discovered in 1941 and dated to 8000 BCE

Over the millennia, a variety of different cultures rose and supplanted one another, with each making a contribution to the evolution of culture in the area. From 6000 to 5200 BCE, the culture known as Kongemose (for the village near a number of 20th-century discoveries) lived in much of modern Denmark. Like the Maglemosians, they were semi-nomadic hunter-gatherer people. Their stone, bone, and wood tools were more advanced than those of the previous culture, and the people had to be quite adaptive since many climatic changes took place during this time. Around 5000 BCE, the last of the Mesolithic (Middle Stone Age) cultures, the Ertebølle, spread in the area (ø sounds like the "u" in burn). The Ertebølle people developed comparatively advanced pottery making and added artistic flourishes to their work. The people of the Ertebølle culture lived not only in Denmark but also in the coastal areas of southern Scandinavia. They began to venture farther into the seas, killing whales and seals with simple harpoons. These early vessels were long canoes around thirty-five feet in length. They were sturdy enough for coastal fishing and also revealed early skills in Scandinavian navigation. Skeletal remains found in Denmark and southern Sweden have been found with arrowheads in them.

We also know that trade existed, at least on a limited and primitive level, as works from the Linear Pottery culture from the Rhine River area of Germany have been found in Denmark. Evidence of food from the northern coastal or riparian areas has been found as well. In the latter part of the Ertebølle culture, their pottery was marked by an increase in decorations, and remnants have been found throughout the area. Archaeologists have also found works from the culture that would replace the Ertebølle in Denmark: the Funnelbeaker culture. Its name comes from their pottery, which was marked by funnels and beaks for easier pouring and decoration.

The Funnelbeaker culture was important since they were the first people to inhabit Denmark, coastal Scandinavia, Germany, and Poland. They made the transition from semi-nomadic hunter-gatherers to a relatively settled farming lifestyle. They raised cattle for milk and meat, and they planted wheat and barley. They also raised pigs, goats, and sheep and used oxen to plow their fields. The Funnelbeaker culture also built early longhouses made of clay with thatched roofs. They were the first people in the area to erect megaliths to mark burial sites of men, women, and children; however, it is not known if these megaliths were marking the importance of the people or not.

The Funnelbeaker culture lasted from c. 4300 to c. 2500 BCE. They were replaced by the Corded Ware culture; they are known for the cord designs on their pottery. Rudimentary defensive works that were put up by the Funnelbeaker people have been found, which strongly suggests internal conflicts were going on while the Corded Ware culture moved in. The Funnelbeaker people soon found themselves at war with more than just themselves. Still, there may have been more than war going on between the two cultural groups, as DNA evidence has suggested that a gene that allows people to digest cow's milk has been found in the three cultures of the area: Linear Pottery, Funnelbeaker, and Corded Ware. Even to this day, southern Europeans are more likely to be lactose intolerant than their northern neighbors.

The Battle Axe Culture

The first people to be recognized as ancestors of the modern Danes (as well as the Swedes, Norwegians, and northern Germans) were from the Battle Axe culture, which appeared in the area around 2800 BCE. This culture was unique for their custom of placing small-to medium-sized stone battle-ax heads in their graves. These graves, unlike those of preceding cultures, were not communal but singular, which means they held only one body. The Battle Axe culture bodies that have been found resemble later Viking Age burials. They were highly standardized, with the men facing east and the women west. The battle-ax heads were placed north to south.

Illustration 2: Small symbolic ax heads found in Battle Axe culture graves. Hundreds of Battle Axe graves have been found in Scandinavia, as well as about three thousand ax heads. *Terker, CC BY 3.0 <https://creativecommons.org/licenses/by/3.0>, via Wikimedia Commons https://commons.wikimedia.org/wiki/File:CordWareBoatAxe.jpg*

The Battle Axe culture's DNA profile included hunter-gatherers from northern Europe, farming cultures from Anatolia (present-day Turkey), and herders from the Eurasian Steppe known as the Yamnaya people.

Another important development at the time of the Battle Axe culture was linguistics. At the time of the Battle Axe people, Indo-European languages were making their way from central Asia and southern Europe into present-day Germany and Scandinavia. At this time, European language branches began to split off. What became the Germanic family of languages developed in the area.

It is fair to say that the likelihood the Battle Axe culture was engaged in violence on a much wider scale than previous cultures was high. Aside from evidence of DNA spreading (which may have come from both consensual and forced sexual encounters), the fact that the battle-ax was so important to these people is likely proof enough. It seems highly unlikely that the ax would've been so venerated if the only thing it was used for was chopping wood.

Chapter 2 – The Nordic Bronze Age

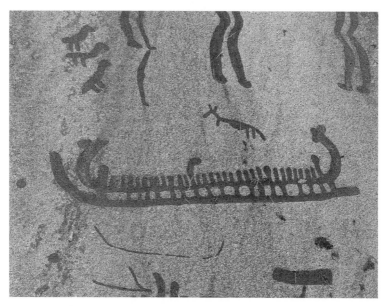

Illustration 3: These petroglyphs in southern Sweden depict events such as raiding and animal domestication during the Nordic Bronze Age. They date from 1700 to 300 BCE and even include a depiction of what is believed to be a blue whale.

https://commons.wikimedia.org/wiki/File:Tanumshede_2005_rock_carvings_7.jpg

The Viking Age is the most famous period of Danish history. Literature (both academic histories and fiction), television shows, movies, and songs (there is a large sub-genre of rock dedicated to songs about or written as Vikings) are full of the same images: violent barbarian raiders who appeared out of nowhere in the late 700s CE. While it may be true that individual Viking raids did seem to appear out of nowhere on the horizon of medieval Britain and France, the Vikings and their raids did not appear "suddenly." In fact, the Viking Age was a culmination of events and developments. One of these was the Nordic Bronze Age, which took place from about 1700 until circa 500 BCE, when it was succeeded by the Iron Age or, more specifically, the Germanic Iron Age. (Iron came to northern Europe later than the rest of Europe.)

As you have read, the cultures occupying Scandinavia used walrus ivory, stone, flint, and wood for their tools and weapons. The development of bronze changed all of that. Bronze is lighter than stone and generally more durable. It's also much more durable than wood, and ivory was also used to make jewelry and other luxury items. With the advent of bronze, more ivory could be used for these highly sought-after and more valuable items. Farming became easier and more productive. For example, farmers could fasten bronze to the end of their plows, leading to deeper and more efficient planting.

Bronze was also used for everyday items, such as cups and cooking pots. Additionally, bronze was highly prized for jewelry and other decorative items. Lastly, bronze was used for weaponry, such as spearheads, swords, axes, and arrowheads. It was lighter, longer-lasting, and easier to hone to a razor-sharp edge.

The problem for the Scandinavians was that there weren't enough of the main elements that went into making bronze: copper and tin.

Illustration 4: Roman cups found in a Bronze Age grave in Denmark.
Leif Plith, Museum Lolland-Falster, CC BY-SA 4.0
<https://creativecommons.org/licenses/by-sa/4.0>, via Wikimedia Commons
https://commons.wikimedia.org/wiki/File:Hoby_b%C3%A6gerne_02_(cropped).jpg

Bronze came to Germanic Europe by way of the Celtic people of central Europe, which were centered on the modern Austrian town (and tourist paradise) of Hallstatt. Known as the Hallstatt culture, the Celtic people had, among other things, a wide-ranging trade network reaching from the Atlantic coast of France to Roman territory and as far east as the Danube in Hungary. For about three hundred years, beginning in about 2000 BCE, the people of what is now northern Germany and Scandinavia traded with the Hallstatt culture for bronze. To "pay" for their bronze tools, weapons, and jewelry, the Scandinavians traded furs, ivory, and amber, which was a highly prized item that was almost impossible to find south of the North and Baltic Seas.

So, you can see that the Nordic Bronze Age marked a point in history for the Scandinavians, as they came into close contact with much of the rest of Europe. They knew of the parts that they did not trade directly with from trading with people who did. It seems as if almost every day for the last few years archaeologists have been finding new and wonderful Roman artifacts in Denmark and the rest of Scandinavia. They were brought there during the Bronze Age, as well as the time that followed (the Vendel period, named after one of the peoples in the area) and into the Viking Age.

Aside from establishing trading connections with other parts of Europe, the people of Scandinavia made the transition from semi-nomadic hunter-gatherers to settled people. Their lives were based on agriculture and the raising of animals, both for food and labor.

So, when did the people who were living in today's Denmark and southern Sweden become "Danes"? The first time that we know of the word "Dane" being used to describe the people in Denmark was in a Roman history of the Gothic peoples of the north. (The Goths were one of the people who originated and dominated the area of Sweden, along with the Svear, whose name lent itself to the name Sweden, in the year 551 CE.) Still, most historians and archaeologists used the term "Germanic" to describe the people of Scandinavia. It was not until about 700 CE that subtle but distinct differences in the people emerged, becoming Danes, Norwegians, and Swedes.

There is one mystery of the Nordic Bronze Age that has yet to be solved to everyone's satisfaction: the mystery of the Jutes. You may remember them from high school or college history courses when studying British history. You were probably told that Britain was invaded by the Angles, Saxons, and Jutes. We know that the Angles and Saxons migrated from areas of today's Germany into coastal Europe, then crossed the English Channel around 400 to 450 CE, around the time Roman rule in Britain was crumbling. At the same time, another Germanic tribe, the Jutes, also made the crossing.

For many years, historians have debated the origin of the Jute tribe. The widely accepted version is that the Jutes hailed from the Jutland Peninsula that makes up most of Denmark; it is believed that the name "Jutland" derives from the tribe's territory. The theory goes that the Jutes were forced out of their territory in approximately 200 CE by another Germanic tribe from southern Sweden: the Danes. They relocated to the Frisian coast (the coast of the present-day Netherlands and northwestern Germany), where they likely came into conflict with the Frisian people, a fierce people group that was frequently in conflict with or joined raids with the Vikings. The Jutes then voyaged to Britain. The Jutes seemed to have settled mainly in the southeastern area of East Anglia and joined with the Angles and the Saxons in their war against the native Britons.

Other historians believe that it's possible the Jutes were actually from Frisia and were pushed out by more dominant tribes. A newer theory holds that the Jutes were from the mountains on the border between Norway and Sweden, northeast of today's Oslo. They moved to greener pastures in Denmark (Jutland) and from there went to Britain. If you can recall your history classes, you might remember that after the Britons had been either killed or pushed into present-day Wales, the Jutes disappeared. They were most likely absorbed through marriage and cultural assimilation by the dominant Angles and Saxons, who merged to become what we know today as the Anglo-Saxons.

Though we don't see the use of the word "Dane" until 550 CE in a Roman work, it is likely that the Danes became a separate people group between 200 and 250 CE, when they separated from the other Germanic tribes living in Sweden and moved to what is now Denmark.

The culture that developed in Denmark, like those in Sweden and Norway, was based on the tribe and the clan. Danish society was divided into three main classes, though some suggest there were more. These were the tribal chieftain and his family, free people, and slaves. Slaves were sometimes traded for or seized from surrounding areas. The Danes "raided" before the Viking Age, though this was done mostly overland.

By the time the Danes became a separate people group, they had developed into fierce warriors whose religious beliefs had already evolved to include the notion that dying a brave death would lead to everlasting life. We have seen how the earlier Battle Axe culture had made a weapon (or a smaller replica of one) into one of the most important symbols of their people; it was so important that people were buried with one in preparation for the next combat-ridden world.

As you may know, the Germanic people that the Romans came into contact with south of Denmark along the Rhine fought differently than they did. The Romans fought in highly disciplined formations and were commanded by non-commissioned officers and commissioned officers. Germanic tribes generally fought en masse, not in disciplined individual formations. They may have been told where to go by their chieftains, but when the battle began, the Germans fought as individuals. While Roman soldiers, of course, recognized an individual's bravery, for the most part, awards or mentions went to the unit, not a man. Germans fought for honor and prestige, both in this world and after. Prowess as a warrior could make a commoner a ruler, as word of his prowess on the battlefield could spread far and wide.

The myths that would develop over time and become today's Norse mythology exalted war, combat prowess, cunning, and bloodshed. The gods watched men as they fought. It is safe to assume that even the most average Germanic warrior was a force to be reckoned with.

Of course, the Danes and other Germanic tribes of the time did not always fight "foreigners" or members of other tribes. Sometimes, disputes between individuals or groups took place. When they did, they were often settled by violence, a certain amount of which was sanctioned by the tribe. However, when this inter-tribal violence threatened to spread, chiefs called for a *thing*. The *thing* was a meeting of all the freemen of the area or tribe; there, problems from food supplies to violent feuds were settled. The *thing* developed long before Viking times, and these meetings have often been depicted in movies and TV shows.

The Germanic longhouse, a communal building, also predated the Viking Age. The longhouse could be the home for the chief and his family, but it was also a communal space where daily matters were discussed, children were communally cared for, and people and animals took shelter during rough weather. There might be a smaller longhouse in a larger village, which would be the home for a local chieftain, and the buildings would grow in size depending on the social stature of the inhabitant and the importance and size of the surrounding settlement.

Though the many Viking-related programs (both dramatic and documentary) today talk about the Viking tradition of cremating a dead warrior in a longship, these "boat-burials" often did not take place at sea. While some of them did include interment in an actual vessel, most of those excavated by archaeologists were boat-shaped stone burial plots.

In either case, the person buried was more than likely an important, powerful, and respected person. Whether a Bronze or Viking Age person, they were surrounded by weapons, treasure, bones, or actual sacrifices. These sacrifices could be animals or people. They were usually slaves, but occasionally, children with finer clothing or jewelry were discovered. This means they were likely a family member who died at the same time, probably from sickness. Most of these burial sites have been found in Norway, though a number have been excavated in Denmark.

Chapter 3 – Vikingr

Vikingr is Old Norse for "Viking" or "Vikings." It is believed by many that a Viking was simply a man who lived in or near a bay, as *vik* is the word for a body of water. It may also have meant someone from the town of Vik in today's Norway, though it's not possible that all Vikings came from that small town on the coast. No matter what its origin, "Viking" has become synonymous with the warriors who began to raid the coasts of western Europe and a large part of western Russia and Ukraine.

For those of you who are unfamiliar with the Vikings and their story, Captivating History's *History of the Vikings* will give you a better overall picture of the Scandinavian warriors. Our purpose here is to give a basic outline of the history of the Danish Vikings. To do that, we will first discuss a couple of things about the Vikings in general before telling the stories of their most well-known leaders.

As we mentioned at the end of the prior chapter, the people of Scandinavia built longhouses for their chieftains and their families. The size of the longhouses seems to have been based on the importance of both the individual ruler and the importance of the settlement they were located in. Naturally, a great king, such as the great Danish Viking Harald Bluetooth (yes, the technology is named for him), would have had a larger longhouse than one of his loyal chieftains in a remote part of Denmark. More than likely, any local leader building a larger longhouse was challenging the overlord and was likely a fool.

In Norway, in 2018, archaeologists discovered the remains of the largest longhouse found so far. It was rebuilt and added to over the years, beginning in about 700 CE, shortly before the Viking Age began. It measures 220 feet long and 33 feet wide. That's more than two-thirds the length of an American football field. We also know that at least some of the Viking elite used lime-based paint to cover the walls of their longhouses. The most widely accepted theory is that this was done to impress visitors. A clean, shining home would imitate the hall of Odin in Valhalla, the afterlife awarded to Vikings slain in battle. The whitewash might also have served to brighten the days and nights of the long Scandinavian winters.

The longhouse was also the center of local Viking life. It would have been used for safety in times of danger (yes, Vikings raided other Vikings), for meetings about communal events, and for a plethora of other things. One thing is for sure, especially in the case of the giant longhouse mentioned above: the great halls of Viking leaders, like the castles and fortresses throughout the world at the time and later, were meant to awe visitors with the owner's power and wealth.

Remember, much of what we know about the Vikings does not come from the Vikings themselves but from firsthand accounts of foreigners (the famous account of Arab traveler Ahmad ibn Fadlan describes his experiences with Swedish Vikings in Russia), secondhand accounts written by Viking enemies (most often by the literate clergy of western Europe, who were certainly biased), and the sagas. The sagas were typically written much later than the events they describe.

More than likely, Viking leaders traveled with a retinue, most of whom were bodyguards, though family members, servants, and slaves would be there as well. From the outside looking in, it makes sense that a Viking lord would travel with berserkers as his bodyguard, but that's probably not what happened. From what we know, the berserkers were likely outcasts in Viking society. While, of course, there were likely famous or esteemed warriors that did go "berserk" in battle, most of those considered to be berserkers were likely antisocial and somewhat dangerous people to be around. They were also unpredictable. In other words, they were not bodyguard material. Accounts of berserkers include them killing their comrades accidentally while in a rage in the heat of battle.

"Berserk" means "bear-shirt." Some believe that these warriors wore actual clothing made from bearskins, which did happen in the cold north. However, what makes the most sense is that the term is a metaphor. When a warrior entered a trance-like state before battle, which was usually brought on by alcohol, bloodlust, or hallucinogenic mushrooms, he put on the "bear-shirt." In other words, he "clothed" himself in the attributes of the bear: he was insanely strong, fast, and vicious. The Ulfhednar, those who became wolves, were considered berserkers; they can be seen in the Netflix series *Vikings: Valhalla.*

Though the longhouse and the berserkers are synonymous with the Vikings, nothing says "Viking" more than the famous Viking longships, sometimes called dragon-ships for the carvings on their prow. Viking longships were fast, had a shallow draft that allowed them to sail upriver, and were purposely made to be flexible, as the Vikings did not want them to easily break apart in rough seas. At the time, the Viking longship was the height of shipbuilding technology, at least in Europe.

We know the warriors from Scandinavia by other names besides Viking. In English and French accounts, they were often referred to as "Northmen" or "Norsemen." The former is an accurate term, as the Vikings came from the north, but the latter name would technically only describe warriors from Norway. Since the words are similar, both today and back then, it is easy to understand the confusion. Besides, no literate monk was going to ask one of the Vikings where they were from and what they preferred to be called. In the heat of the moment,

Danes became Norsemen, and Norsemen became Danes. The Swedes were often called "Rus" from the Finnish word *Ruotsi*, meaning "rowers." (However, some believe the word "Rus" comes from the inhabitants of what is now Russia, who called the Swedes "red" for their red hair, beards, and ruddy complexions.)

The Danish Vikings raided mostly to the west—the eastern coast of England and France. However, it's more than likely that, given the close ties between Viking clans in different areas, there were Danes on Swedish voyages to the south and on Norse raids to the northeastern and western parts of England, Ireland, and Scotland.

The popular TV series *Vikings* depict Ragnar Lothbrok (Lodbrok), a legendary Viking chieftain, as a Norwegian whose home was Kattegat, the name of a body of water that lies between Denmark and Sweden. (Ragnar may or may not have existed; it is thought that Ragnar may have been a conglomeration of many Viking legends.) Dane and Swedish legends have it that Björn Ironside was one of Ragnar's sons. Therefore, it's highly doubtful that the Great Heathen Army was motivated by vengeance for the murder of Ragnar. It was more of a giant war party whose aim was not merely riches but also settlement and perhaps the conquest of England itself.

As you likely know, the Anglo-Saxons of Wessex under Alfred the Great (r. 871–899) and his descendants were, at one time, the only Anglo-Saxon kingdom left in England. For a time, the Danes and a number of Norwegians ruled East Anglia, Mercia, and Northumberland. This was the famous Danelaw, the territory in which Danish law was prominent.

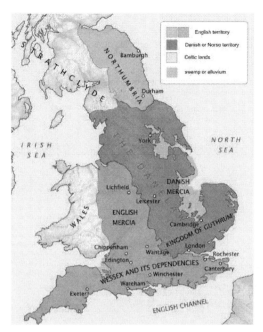

Illustration 5: This simple map gives a good idea of the extent of the Danelaw. In Scotland and the area around Liverpool and Chester, the Norsemen seem to have been more numerous than their Danish brethren.

Hel-hama, CC BY-SA 3.0 https://creativecommons.org/licenses/by-sa/3.0 via Wikimedia Commons; https://commons.wikimedia.org/wiki/File:England_878.svg

Who were some of the more famous Danish Vikings? One of them was Guthrum (c. 835-890). Although Guthrum is depicted in the Netflix series *The Last Kingdom* as a treacherous and disloyal man, he was likely no more disloyal than any other Viking of the time. He was a leader in two armies. A large raiding force took place in the spring and early summer of 871 known as the Great Summer Army, and it joined forces with the famous Great Heathen Army, which had landed in England five years before and was waging a campaign to take over England.

Guthrum was a nephew of the Danish King Horik II, and he likely was an accomplished warrior in his own right. By the time he met up with the Great Heathen Army, Guthrum was thirty-five, which was relatively old, both in general for the time and specifically for a Viking warrior. In the winter of 878, Guthrum led a surprise attack on

Alfred's court at Chippenham, which was a great defeat for the English. Alfred was forced to take to the marshes for safety.

Unfortunately for Guthrum, he was captured at the Battle of Edington later in 878. He was forced to convert to Christianity to save his life and status, and he was eventually given lands in East Anglia, which he governed for Alfred. He also had to fight future Viking raiders should they come. Guthrum's Christian name was Æthelstan (for those of you familiar with the series *Vikings*, Æthelstan, an English monk, was a main character for the first three seasons). Guthrum maintained peace in his area, though isolated raids did occur. He must have been greatly respected since he was recognized by both the English and Northmen as the "king" (under Alfred) of East Anglia.

A similar situation occurred in France some forty years later. This one involved the famed Rollo, who is also a main character in *Vikings*. Rollo's name in Old Norse is Hrolf Ganger, which means "Hrolf the Walker," as he was reputed to be so tall that he could not sit on a horse without his feet dragging on the ground (hence, he walked). Most evidence points to Rollo being a Dane, though many believe he may have been Norse. In 911, King Charles the Bald of France gave Rollo and his warriors land in what became Normandy ("land of the Northmen") to bribe them to stop raiding and defend France. Rollo's great-grandson, Richard II, would be the first official duke of Normandy about one hundred years later.

In the early 900s, the English began a campaign to take back the land under Danish law. In 954, the last Danish king in England, the treacherous Eric Bloodaxe, was killed in battle. While the Danelaw still existed under local Danish rulers, they all swore fealty and paid taxes to the English king, who at this time was Eadred (r. 946-955).

This situation lasted until 1002 when English king Æthelred the Unready (when translated from Old English, his actually means ill-advised, not unprepared) decided to launch a campaign on St. Brice's Day (November 2nd) to eliminate all of the Northmen in England.

Today, this is known as genocide. His desire to do this didn't come out of thin air. The Viking raids had increased, but Æthelred was also deeply into spreading the Christian faith. He also sought to rule all of England without Danish help. Æthelred's forces killed an estimated twenty to thirty thousand Danes and Norwegians. One of the dead was the sister of a Danish king with a formidable reputation named Sweyn Forkbeard.

For the next ten years, Sweyn and his men, as well as other Vikings who were encouraged by Sweyn and the promise of great riches, land, and vengeance, raided England with increasing ferocity. With the help of English ealdormen, who changed sides due to bribes, dissatisfaction with Æthelred's rule, and/or threats, Sweyn took control of London and the area around it. Sweyn's son, Cnut, would go on to even greater heights and become known as Cnut the Great (c. 994–1035). Many times, especially in accounts written in the 19th and early 20th centuries, Cnut (or Canute) is depicted as something of a madman, standing or sitting at the edge of the ocean as the tide rolled in. Cnut became the master of not only Denmark but also England, Norway, and parts of Sweden. His power was unrivaled, and the early stories say that Cnut stood in front of the waves, commanding them to recede, only to be disappointed that his power was not *that* great. However, the more likely story, which is still probably apocryphal, has Cnut going to the water's edge to show the earls and generals around him that his power *was* limited, no matter how much they might believe otherwise.

Cnut was not a madman; he knew the limits of his power, which was indeed immense. After the death of his father, the English king Æthelred was invited to return to England by his former ealdormen and the first Norwegian king to convert to Christianity, Olaf Haraldsson. Olaf led an attack on London Bridge and then helped drive out the Danes from London and the area around it, which was their stronghold in England. Cnut, who had become the master of London after his father's death, decided to return to Denmark and solidify his rule there but not before massacring his English hostages and leaving them to rot on the beach as a warning.

In that same year, 1015, Cnut returned with a large fleet of two hundred ships and perhaps ten thousand men. Over the next year, Æthelred's heir, Edmund II (sometimes known as Edmund Ironside for his success in repelling a number of Danish attacks), and Cnut waged a vicious war for control of England. Æthelred died in April 1016, making Edmund the new king. In October, Cnut and Edmund fought the vicious Battle of Assandun in Essex. Though Cnut and the Danes were victorious, it was a costly battle, and Edmund vowed to continue the fight. With this being the case, Cnut and Edmund came up with a reasonable solution: Edmund would rule Wessex (the area south of the Thames River, at least generally speaking), and Cnut would rule the rest of England.

For Cnut, the only problem left in England was the territory of Northumbria, which had formerly been a kingdom but was now an earldom under the English king. However, the earl of Northumbria, Uhtred, refused to recognize Cnut's authority. Cnut's allies assassinated Uhtred in his own hall, and Cnut ruled all of England except Wessex. (You might recognize some of the strands of the story from Bernard Cornwell's books on Viking Age England and Netflix's interpretation of them in *The Last Kingdom*). In late November 1016, Edmund II died, and Cnut, with the support of the English lords in Wessex, became the king of England shortly after.

Cnut's early rule was marked by actions that could only be described as "Viking" in nature. He gave a sizable amount of land that had been taken from the English nobles to his Danish allies. He also had Edmund's brother, Eadwig, killed; a number of Englishmen were killed, as Cnut believed they might give him trouble in the future. One of these men was the powerful Mercian lord Eadric Streona, who had turned against his kinsmen to join Cnut and then seemed to engage in plots to make himself king.

One of the Viking chieftains allied with Cnut was known as Thorkell the Tall, and he was given authority over East Anglia. Thorkell was a member of the Jomsvikings, which can best be described as a Viking version of the later Knights Templar, an order of fanatic Christian knights that rose to prominence in the 1100s. The Jomsvikings were reputed to be fanatic believers in the Norse gods and were some of the greatest warriors at the time. Eventually, the Jomsvikings were defeated in 1043 by Magnus I of Norway, as they had become less of a religious military order and more mercenary in nature. They had contributed to a lot of instability in the region.

Thorkell was apparently an untrustworthy and/or power-hungry man. He had aided Æthelred in his conflict against Sweyn Forkbeard and then switched sides to aid Cnut. By 1021, Thorkell had apparently begun to plot to become king himself. He was removed from power by Cnut and sent back to Denmark, where he died shortly thereafter.

By 1018, Cnut had either distributed enough English lands or paid off his men to their satisfaction. In that year, a new chapter in England began. Cnut began to entrust more of his realm to English nobles, and Englishmen outnumbered Danes on his privy council. Cnut also maintained English laws and traditions in the country and his court. When he needed English help to put down problems in Denmark in 1019, he got it. In 1027, he and Scottish King Malcolm I came to terms. The Scots recognized Cnut's overlordship of their land, but he never truly ruled their country.

In Denmark, in 1026, Cnut's brother-in-law, Ulf, attempted to seize control, uniting with Swedish and Norwegian lords to do so. Through warfare, diplomacy, and bribes, Cnut managed to gain control of lands in southern Sweden and all of Norway. One of the most famous battles of the later Viking Age was between the forces of Cnut and those of Norwegian King Olaf Haraldsson. At the Battle of Stiklestad on the Norwegian coast, Olaf was defeated. After being wounded, he fell off the prow of his ship and succumbed to the waves.

Cnut titled himself the "King of all England and Denmark, and the Norwegians, and some of the Swedes." What was known as the Great Northern Empire was created, though it did not survive long after Cnut's death in 1035.

Cnut is remembered, not only in Denmark but also in England, as a wise and fair king. And by all accounts, this seems to be true. Adding to his prestige was his meeting in Rome with the pope and the Holy Roman emperor, where he was seen as an equal, at least in terms of temporal (earthly) power.

Cnut died in 1035 and was succeeded by his son Harald, which is usually spelled the English way as "Harold." He ruled for a short five years and was followed by Cnut's youngest son, Harthacnut, in 1040. Harthacnut was not his father; during his reign, the Danish rule in England weakened. When Cnut the Great died, the son of Olaf Haraldsson, Magnus I, became the king of Norway, depriving Harthacnut of a large portion of his kingdom. Harthacnut died in 1042; he was the last Viking king of England. The English put forward Edward the Confessor, the son of Æthelred and Emma of Normandy. She had married Cnut after the English king's death, making Edward Harthacnut's half-brother. Edward was one of the last Anglo-Saxon kings of England, dying in 1066, shortly before the Norman Conquest.

The Great Northern Empire of Cnut the Great was short-lived, but it illustrates the power of Denmark, which would only continue to grow in the next several hundred years.

Chapter 4 – Christianity

Since the time of the great Frankish Emperor Charlemagne (r. 800–814), the Danes and other people in northern and central Europe had had to deal with the expansion of Christianity. Charlemagne sought to eradicate pagan beliefs from most of Germany. Some historians consider Charlemagne's wars against the Saxons to be genocide, as likely tens of thousands were killed during the Frankish emperor's campaign. Many others were forced to convert at the tip of a spear, and anyone caught reverting to their pagan ways would suffer a grisly death. It even got to the point where Christianized children reported on parents and other relatives.

By the 900s, most of Germany and parts of today's Austria and Poland had been Christianized by the Franks. Fortunately for the Danes, Charlemagne's sons and later descendants were too concerned with fighting each other than to carry out the Christianization of Denmark. That was not the only factor, though. By the time of Charlemagne's death, the Danes and other Scandinavians had become a mighty force that terrorized much of Europe from the 800s onward. This means the Frankish kings had little time or ability to worry about making Denmark and Norway Christian.

In England, the Vikings' numbers matched well against the divided forces of the Anglo-Saxons. But they would have little hope against a united Frankish empire determined to spread Christianity. The Franks outnumbered the Danes, and the Vikings were not equipped to deal with a full-fledged land campaign on the border of their homeland.

To keep the enemy at bay while they raided, the Danish Vikings took the prudent step of building fortifications throughout the southern part of their homeland. In the late 7th century, the Danes began building what has become known as the Danevirke (Danework), a series of deep trenches, walls, and the occasional tower to keep the Danes safe from an attack from the south. Over the centuries, until the late 1800s, the Danevirke was added to, eventually becoming a formidable line of defense. Only the coming of modern warfare in the mid-1800s made it obsolete.

Within Denmark and southern Sweden, which may at the time have been "Danish," we know of seven Danish ring fortresses, which are also known by the Old Norse name Trelleborg ("fort built by slaves"). These forts have been dated to the Viking era, specifically during the reign of Harald Bluetooth (r. c. 958–986). These fortresses were quite large and peopled not only by warriors stationed there to guard the territory but also by their families, livestock, and slaves. These fortresses might have had intimidating armies, but they were likely a magnet for traders from other regions of Europe. They also attracted missionaries.

At first, there was just a trickle of monks traveling into Denmark. Some were never heard from again, at least at the beginning of the Viking Age. Later, as the Scandinavians became more exposed to Christian people and ideas and as their contact with more of Europe increased, a number of Vikings converted to the new faith.

Arguably one of, if not the most, successful Viking of all, Cnut the Great, was Christian, although he did not hesitate to war with other Christians when it was to his advantage. Just a short time before Cnut's rise, the idea of a Christian Viking would have been an oxymoron, but by the first decade of the 2nd millennium, more and more Vikings were converting. For some, Christianity, with its tale of a resurrected son of an all-powerful being, sounded familiar to the Norse. In Norse mythology, Baldur, the son of Odin, the All-Father and supreme deity of the Viking universe, was said to rise again after his death set in motion Ragnarök, the final battle between light and darkness. After the gods and the forces of darkness (giants, the goddess of death, and the damned who died a coward's death) had destroyed themselves, Baldur would be resurrected as the god of light, and a new age would begin. Some Scandinavians based their conversion to the new religion on this, and it was a notion that many of the monks were more than happy to let the Vikings believe. (As a side note, conversion was a much easier process in Denmark and Sweden than it was in Norway, where it took another one hundred years and much more bloodshed.)

The first Danish king to convert was the aforementioned Harald Bluetooth, who likely improved the Danevirke and built a number of the ring fortresses. He eventually converted in the 960s. By the time he did, a large segment of the population was already Christian and, for the most part, existed side by side. One archaeological discovery that helped advance this idea was a blacksmith's mold dating from the period, which could make crosses and Thor's hammer.

A number of theories exist about why Harald Bluetooth chose that moment in time to convert. Some say that he had become a true believer, that he actually continued to believe in the "old ways" while acting Christian, or that he did so for political and economic reasons. Christianity seemed to be dominant in Europe. The Christian nations were powerful and more technologically advanced, especially in regard to architecture. But perhaps most importantly, these countries seemed to be tremendously wealthy.

Raiding could bring you quick riches, but raiding was much less regular and more costly than trading. Many people are under the impression that the Scandinavians of the Viking Age were either raiders/warriors or farmers. We know that some of the largest trading centers in northern Europe were off the coast of Sweden and

Denmark and that Scandinavia was economically tied to places as far away as India and possibly China. Within Europe, trading with other Christians seemed to bring better terms and an early form of "most favored nation" status for its traders and kings.

Over the course of the next century, the Danes rapidly converted to Christianity. To many in the country, the tide seemed to have turned against the old gods, as those who held on to the old ways found it in their best interest (economically, militarily, and spiritually) to move on from Thor, Odin, Freya, and the rest. In Sweden, a relatively similar process occurred. Despite some incidents, on the whole, Sweden's conversion, like Denmark's, was relatively peaceful, especially when compared to the conversion process in Norway, which included civil war, forced conversions, and violence on a large scale. The Norwegians didn't become a Christian kingdom until the 1100s.

Chapter 5 – Margaret, Queen of Denmark, Norway, and Sweden

The Viking Age came to a rather abrupt end in 1066 when the last great Viking warrior, Norwegian Harald Hardrada ("hard ruler"), attempted to assert his very tenuous claim to the English crown upon the death of Edward the Confessor. Harold Godwinson defeated Hardrada. It is believed that Harold Godwinson was named Edward's successor on his deathbed. Unfortunately for Harold, he had previously sworn to the duke of Normandy, William, that he would honor William's own claim to the English throne while he was William's "guest" in Normandy after a shipwreck on the Norman coast. But after returning to England, Harold forgot all about his promise and moved to make himself king, necessitating William's successful invasion. Harold would die in the famous Battle of Hastings, marking a new age in England.

In the years between 1066 and the formation of the Kalmar Union, which consisted of Denmark, Norway, and Sweden, in 1397, Denmark began to withdraw back into itself. When the Danes lost England after the death of Harthacnut, Norway separated, and only a part of southern Sweden belonged to Denmark. By the 1100s, Denmark had turned inward to a degree, though it did become tremendously wealthy due to its position as the "gatekeeper" of the Baltic Sea. Denmark also benefited, at least for much of the time, from being closely involved and located near the growing economic powerhouse cities of northern Germany, which began to rise to prominence in the late 1100s. These independent German city-states would unite in one of the world's first commercial trading blocs. They were known as the Hanseatic League, and it would both support and war against Denmark in the coming centuries.

By the middle to the late 1300s, Denmark was still a power to be reckoned with, but its direct influence was not felt throughout Europe as it once had. With the Danish kingdom reduced in size (though it did hold lands in southern Sweden, which were populated mostly by Danes and, to an extent, German traders), most of its international affairs had two purposes. The Danes wanted to make money, which was becoming more difficult due to competition from the Hanseatic League, and prevent other powers, such as England, Russia, and the Hanseatic League (which had armies and navies of its own, including well-paid mercenaries), from reducing Denmark's power and territory.

Margaret (or Margrethe) was destined to unite the Scandinavian people, but not in the way her father had envisioned. Her father, King Valdemar IV of Denmark, knew, like so many rulers, that a noblewoman's value came not from anything she achieved herself but from the connections, wealth, and potential children she could bring to a union. Most marriages in the Middle Ages, at least within the European nobility, were not matters of love but of politics. A local chief might marry his daughter to a neighbor and rival in order to end a feud or gain access to land. It was not that different at the top of society: kings and queens married their daughters off to gain a political advantage. If their daughter was both pretty and knowledgeable, it was easy to make a match. Most of the time, pretty was good enough. Wars could be ended or new alliances made to gain an advantage. Riches for a much-sought-after princess would change hands. The boundaries of territories might change, and new kingdoms formed that would change world history.

Initially, that was Margaret I of Denmark's role to play. She was betrothed at the age of ten to Haakon VI of Norway, who was sixteen years her senior. There was no expectation of any sort of physical intimacy until after the marriage, and Margaret stayed with her father until she became of child-bearing age.

Margaret's marriage to Haakon was intended to place the three Scandinavian countries under one crown. Haakon was the son of Magnus IV Eriksson (the Swedish royal naming protocol has the number before the last name), who was the king of Norway and Sweden. At the time, Sweden did not include all of the Scandinavian Peninsula as we know it today, as this was Danish territory. It was expected that Haakon would become king after the death of Valdemar IV.

The union of the ruling houses of Denmark with that of Sweden and Norway would also put one of Denmark's and Valdemar's rivals, the noble family of Mecklenburg, into contention for the Swedish throne. No matter how careful one is, something unexpected usually happens. In this case, the Swedish nobility, who had a say in who became the king, did not want to take the chance with Magnus and find themselves under Danish control. At the time, Denmark was a more powerful and prosperous kingdom than Sweden, and many Danish kings had had their eyes on conquering Sweden.

So, the Swedish nobles on the royal council forced Magnus out and invited Albrecht of Mecklenburg to become the Swedish king. Unfortunately for Denmark, Valdemar, who had reunited Denmark when it had defaulted on its debts and was temporarily under the sway of the Hanseatic League, was not a popular man. The Swedes allied with the Norwegians, some Danish nobles, and the Hansa (a common term referring to the Hanseatic League). They forced Valdemar to relinquish certain rights he had unilaterally imposed on the passage from the Baltic to the North Sea (this included taxes, tolls, fishing rights, and right of passage, among other things). The Hanseatic League also forced Valdemar to give it certain commercial rights in Denmark and a say in the succession to the Danish throne. The Danes were not happy about this outcome. By the time of his death in 1375, Valdemar had succeeded in putting down a number of rebellions in Jutland and was in the process of making an ally out of Pope Gregory IX in order to strengthen his position and that of his dynasty. However, he passed away on October 24th before he could make that a reality.

When Valdemar died, his daughter Margaret maneuvered behind the scenes to get her son Olaf named the king of Denmark. The political skill Margaret showed to get her son named king should have been (and probably was) a sign that she was a force to be reckoned with. On top of that, Margaret arranged to have herself named regent, and she ruled Denmark from that point onward, even after the death of her son and the adoption of her sister's eldest son, who became Eric VII. Margaret was the true power behind the throne in Denmark.

Some historians have called her the first great queen of Europe, but for many years, she was overlooked and ranked under other great European queens, most notably Elizabeth I of England and Isabella I of Spain. While she might not have world-shaking effects like these other women, Margaret managed to stabilize an unstable region and unite the Scandinavian people together in a union that lasted into the 19th century (albeit in different forms). Margaret was intelligent and had the best education available to a woman of the time. She also must have been a keen observer and quick learner, as she spent her years before joining Haakon in true marriage watching and listening to the palace intrigues in Denmark. She observed the ebb and flow of war and became acquainted with the men in power.

In 1387, Margaret and her son Olaf were about to launch an attack on Sweden on the basis of what they believed were better claims to the Swedish throne than what Albrecht of Mecklenburg had. By this time, Olaf had come of age and ruled with his mother. However, just before the invasion was to be launched, Olaf died of a mysterious illness. (In 2021, an excellent Danish movie, *Margaret, Queen of the North*, was made. It includes the story of the "false" Olaf, a pretender who asserted that he was Olaf and that he had never died; much more is made of this story in the movie than occurred in real life, however.)

When Olaf died, Margaret adopted her sister's son and was named regent of both Denmark and Norway. During 1387 and 1388, Margaret worked with disenchanted Swedish nobles who were angry at Albrecht, as he had given their lands to his allies and Germans from the Hanseatic League. The Swedish nobles joined Margaret and named her Sweden's "sovereign lady and rightful ruler." A war with Albrecht was inevitable. Although Albrecht was strong in the southeast of the country and on Sweden's islands in the Baltic, he was ultimately defeated. He was captured by Margaret's forces and held prisoner until the forces loyal to him surrendered six years later.

By 1389, Margaret was the ruler of Denmark, Norway, and Sweden (as well as Finland, which was a Swedish possession). Being a monarch in the 14th and 15th centuries was not easy, and that goes double for a woman with actual power. Though Margaret was called insulting names, sometimes even in front of her by opposing nobles (such as King Breechless or "King without pants"), she was admired by many and inspired loyalty. There were other names that were not so denigrating, such as Lady King and Semiramis of the North, the latter of which is derived from a legendary queen of Babylon.

In 1396, Eric was declared king, but all the power rested in the hands of Margaret. At Kalmar, located on the coast of southern Sweden, the queen attempted to forge an official union of the Scandinavian countries in 1397. Each would have a king that would act as a governor of their respective countries, but Margaret would be the overlord or empress, so to speak (this word was not used, though). One of the issues that were left unsettled was whether the kings would follow the laws and customs of their own countries or be told what to do by Margaret. This was never settled to anyone's full satisfaction, but as long as the kings were responsive to the military needs of the Kalmar Union, Margaret did not mind too much if the kings oversaw local laws.

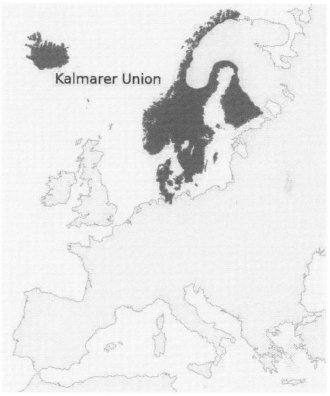

Illustration 6: The Kalmar Union at the beginning of the 16th century.
NordNordWest, CC BY-SA 3.0 https://creativecommons.org/licenses/by-sa/3.0 via Wikimedia Commons; https://commons.wikimedia.org/wiki/File:Kalmar_Union_c._1500-de.svg

The Kalmar Union was declared when Eric was made king of Denmark, Norway, and Sweden on June 17th, 1397. The union was a tremendous achievement for the time. For all intents and purposes, it ended when the Swedes under Gustav I Vasa (considered the "Father of Modern Sweden") rebelled and successfully split Sweden from the union and became the Swedish king in his own right in 1523. Though Norway eventually became more of Denmark's vassal than a partner, the Kalmar Union, at least in name, continued through 1814, which was when Sweden took Norway. In 1905, Norway split from Sweden.

Although the Kalmar Union had been dead in any real sense since the 1500s, all traces of the union ended at that time.

From the time of the Kalmar Union until the day Margaret died in 1412, she had gradually assumed more and more power. She limited the power of the nobility, especially in Denmark, and gained great power in the country by establishing a system of local sheriffs and constabularies to keep order and keep an eye on potential enemies. She also levied taxes on some church properties, which at the time was almost unheard of, although she maintained good relations with the pope. She also worked hard to limit the influence and power of the Hanseatic League, whose cities were on or close to the Danish border. Just before her death, she entered into a war with the Duchy of Holstein, a much-disputed territory before her time and long after she was gone. Margaret died before the war ended.

Today, Margaret is seen as a great uniter of the people, though she was authoritarian at times (it's almost impossible to see her succeeding back then without being so). Today's Danish queen took the name Margaret (or Margarethe in Danish) at her coronation in honor of the "Lady King."

Chapter 6 – Christian II

A bit more than one hundred years after Margaret's death, the Kalmar Union, at least as she had envisioned and formed it to be, ceased to exist. There were a number of problems with the union. First, Scandinavia is huge, spanning thousands of miles—and that's just the coastline. At the time, it was not possible to know with any certainty or swiftness what was happening in every corner of the union.

Second, the kings of each nation, barring Denmark, might have felt their interests did not side with Danish interests. One of the biggest reasons for Sweden's break from the Kalmar Union had to do with Denmark's interactions with the Hanseatic League. Denmark bordered or was near many Hanseatic cities and had many economic interactions with them. The relationship between Denmark and the Hansa was a balancing act and sometimes led to bloodshed. However, in Sweden, which was farther away from the Hansa, there was resentment. The Hansa merchants had become quite powerful in Sweden and had even been granted their own lands by various kings at the expense of Swedish noble families. In some places, German merchants were essentially governing Swedish towns, which was much resented. Additionally, the Swedes felt they had enough economic clout on their own due to commodities like furs, endless timber, and amber that no one else had. They did not want to go through Hansa middlemen and wanted the profits for themselves. They also did not want to be dragged into a war because the Danes and the Hansa demanded it.

Third, despite the similarities in language and culture, the Danes, the Swedes, and the Norwegians were not the same people. They had their own customs and traditions. While the Kalmar Union did not attempt to change those customs, the fact that Sweden was ruled by a Danish ruler often made the Swedes feel like second-class citizens.

When Margaret died, her nephew, Eric VII, became the true king of the Kalmar Union. However, he was unpopular, especially in Sweden, where a rebellion caused the nobles of all three countries to force him off the throne in 1439. For about ten years, the local lords ruled their countries, but disorder and disagreement about the succession forced a temporarily but weak reunion of Kalmar with Norway. This first happened under Christopher of Bavaria, who had family ties in Denmark, and continued until Christian II became the king of Denmark.

Christian II is one of the most controversial kings in Danish history for a number of reasons, which we will discuss in a moment, but his main claim to history was his determination to reform the Kalmar Union as it had existed during Margaret's time. To do that, he had to conquer Sweden. At the time of his enthronement as the king of Denmark and Norway, Sweden was in a state of near civil war, with various nobles vying for the throne or increased power. A number of them wished to rejoin the union, but to do so would cause a full-blown civil war in the country. When Christian was crowned, the Swedish delegation was asked what their position was. They replied, "We have the choice between peace at home and strife here, or strife at home and peace here—we choose the former." The question of who would be the king of Sweden would be postponed until the Swedes decided on a king for themselves, accepted Christian as their monarch, or were conquered by the Danes. They could not do the former, would not do the latter, and Christian began his campaign against Sweden in 1517.

Within Sweden, two main factions existed. One faction was the anti-Danish faction, which consisted of nobles and their followers led by the powerful regent Sten Sture the Younger, who had ambitions to become king himself. Opposing them was the faction that supported uniting with Denmark. This faction was led by Archbishop Gustav Trolle.

Illustration 7: Romantic Era painting of Christian II and his mistress Dyveke Sigbritsdatter, a commoner whose mother became the king's advisor after her daughter's death. Christian was married to Isabella of Austria, with whom he had three children.
https://commons.wikimedia.org/wiki/File:DyvekeSigbritsdochter.jpg

To strengthen his position, both within Sweden and with the Catholic Church, Christian asked for the support and blessing of Pope Leo X, who came from the powerful and wealthy Medici family of Florence, Italy. With the pope's help, Christian put together an invasion fleet in 1517 and sailed for Sweden to relieve the siege of the archbishop's fortress. Christian was defeated, and what's more, he was humiliated; many of Sture's men were peasant levies, not the professional or semi-professional soldiers that Christian had brought with him. The next year, Christian was back again with another fleet and thousands of soldiers. Once again, he was defeated, this time at the bloody Battle of Brännkyrka near Stockholm.

By 1520, Christian had amassed an even larger fleet. In addition to Danish soldiers, he hired a number of mercenaries from France, the German states (Germany was not a country until 1871), and Scotland. Christian was victorious in two battles: the Battle of Bogesund on a frozen lake in January in which Sten Sture was killed and a follow-up battle near the important Swedish royal city of Uppsala. A long siege of Stockholm led by Sten Sture's widow and consequent negotiations caused Christian to accede to the wishes of the Swedish nobles, agreeing that Sweden should be governed according to Swedish law and customs.

This is where things get really interesting, and it is where Christian made a fatal error, at least as far as his future as the king went. Three days after Christian's coronation as king of Sweden, the king's ally, Archbishop Trolle, declared that all of the nobles who had opposed him during the war were heretics and needed to be brought to trial for their "crimes" against the church. Christian, who was naturally paranoid and a cruel man to begin with, saw this as an opportunity to cement his rule in Sweden for the foreseeable future.

Christian summoned all of the nobles who had followed Sten Sture to a meeting at Stockholm Castle for the long festivities celebrating his coronation. Sten Sture, who had died at the battle on the lake in 1520, was declared a heretic. By custom, those who had sworn an oath to Sture were, therefore, declared as guilty as their leader. They were arrested on the spot, and over the course of two days, eighty to one hundred Swedish nobles and village elders were beheaded or hanged, including two bishops who had been enemies of Archbishop Trolle. This should have gotten Christian into hot water with the pope, who was his supporter, but the king blamed the deaths on soldiers who had "gotten out of hand." This episode in Scandinavian history has been referred to as the "Stockholm Massacre" ever since.

One of the victims of the massacre was Erik Johansson Vasa, a nobleman from north-central Sweden. His son was Gustav I Vasa. Gustav was a man of immense strength, cunning, and determination. He eventually defeated Christian in the Swedish War of Liberation (1521–1523). Today, he is known in Sweden as the "Father of Modern Sweden."

Christian was an interesting man. Although he was undoubtedly murderous, he was also a man with a keen intellect. However, certain reforms got him in hot water with the Danish nobles, who eventually rebelled and forced Christian into a relatively luxurious exile in the castles of Sønderborg and Kalundborg.

In 1521, while Gustav Vasa was busy in the hinterlands of Sweden putting together an army, Christian II visited the Netherlands, which was, as it is now, one of the most modern European nations. He even met the great philosopher Erasmus and secretly converted to Protestantism, though he reverted to Catholicism upon his return to Denmark four months later.

When Christian returned to his kingdom, he issued two royal edicts: the Town Law and the Land Law. The Town Law reorganized the trading system in Denmark, which was only to be done in the towns (as opposed to on nobles' lands or homes, for example). The towns were to be governed by the king's appointees. This also made tax collection both easier and faster. Additionally, the Town Law forbade nobles from selling or trading peasants. (Since the late 1100s and early 1200s, peasants had been treated almost like slaves in Denmark, as they were tied forever to the land they were born on and had no real rights). The peasants were also given the right to negotiate their terms of tenure (how long they would work and wages, for example) with the nobility. Though it was designed to weaken the nobility, Christian's Town Law was an early step toward real reforms.

It should be known that Christian's mistress and her mother were both commoners, which likely had an effect on Christian's attitude toward the peasant class.

The Land Law was likely a result of Christian's visit to the Netherlands and his exposure to the ideas of Lutheranism and Protestantism. Christian declared that priests could marry in Denmark, and some rights of the church were taken over by the state. Though the peasants and traders of Denmark approved of these reforms (Christian was known by some as "Christian the Good"), the powerful nobles and higher clergy did not.

Worse still, as far as Christian's position as king was concerned, he raised tolls on traffic through the many waterways controlled by Denmark that led to the North Sea and the Atlantic. Some of those who had to pay tolls came from the powerful Hanseatic cities of Lübeck (almost on the Danish border) and Danzig (on today's Polish coast). These cities allied themselves with Gustav I Vasa in Sweden and, in combination with the disenchanted Danish nobles, finally overthrew Christian. They voted in a new king (this time just of Denmark and Norway), Frederick (Frederik) I, who reigned for nearly ten years until 1533.

Chapter 7 – The Protestant Reformation in Denmark

During the Late Middle Ages, the European economies grew at an amazing rate. The establishment of the double-entry ledger (which counted not just the inflow but also the outflow of wealth), the expansion of trade through the building of roads and canals, and the beginning of the international credit system meant that Europe, especially western Europe, was becoming vastly wealthy.

With that wealth came a higher standard of living, more institutions of higher learning, and, of course, corruption. Corruption had been an age-old problem, but with the immense wealth being amassed, individuals and families could buy positions of power or even rise to rule a kingdom. You have already read about this happening with the Hanseatic League, which was an economic union of a number of northern European cities (mostly German, but there were also Dutch and Polish areas) that banded together for both profit and protection. From the 1300s to the early 1500s, the Hansa cities became powerful enough to tip the balance of war and even make or break kings. Though the Hansa cities were not corporations as we know them today, the Hanseatic traders and others, such as the famous Dutch East India Company, had many similarities to today's business world.

Making business even more profitable was the development of the early stock market in Antwerp in 1531. This idea quickly spread throughout northern Europe and increased profits.

These ideas, along with the discovery of the Western Hemisphere, increased trade, and colonization in Asia, allowed even small countries like the Netherlands to become amazingly rich. Denmark also became wealthy; its control of the many straits leading out of the Baltic gave it power and riches beyond its size. And combined with modern developments like corporations (the Danish East India Company, which began in 1616, is one example) and credit systems, the control of the Danish Straits made Denmark one of the more wealthy and powerful countries in Europe, at least until the early 1600s.

With all of this wealth, there is no wonder that corrupt and greedy individuals took as much advantage of the economy as they could. For many honest individuals, especially in the rising middle class of Europe, the corruption was tolerable, if not excessive. At times, riots and uprisings by the middle or lower classes erupted. Although these disturbances sometimes resulted in change, they often ended with the rioters being put down harshly, at times with barbaric violence.

While corruption among the upper classes and the newly developed non-noble upper middle classes (such as the Medici in Florence and the Fuggers and Rothschilds in today's Germany) was common and more or less expected, it was difficult to tolerate corruption in the Catholic Church. Though much of eastern Europe was Orthodox Christian, its unity, influence, and power were not as great as that of the Catholic Church, which had an elaborate organization under the rule of the pope. The pope was (and still is) seen as the representative of Christ on Earth by Catholics. There were also Christian sects, such as the Copts, in places like Egypt and Ethiopia, but they were much smaller in both believers and power than the church in Europe.

That being said, for all of western and central Europe, the Catholic Church was the *only* church. Economists will tell you that when a person or group of people has absolute control of the market, corruption (both in terms of economics and power) occurs. The Catholic Church had grown in power since the legalization of Christianity by Roman Emperor Constantine in 313 CE. To the Europeans, the Catholic Church was the only way to reach heaven.

For centuries, the popes in Rome had rivaled the great kings and queens in power and wealth. Corruption had always existed, but by the early 1500s, people throughout Europe were questioning not only the church's behavior but also its monopoly on God. You see, the Bible and all other important Christian documents were written in Latin. Sermons were delivered in only Latin. After the demise of the Western Roman Empire in the 400s, more and more people began to speak their own national languages and not Latin. Latin became the language of diplomacy and the upper classes (for a time), and it was the only language in which the Word of God was printed. Parishioners had to take it on faith that their priest or bishop was teaching them the Bible's lessons correctly. The people could not generally access the Bible for themselves, even if they were a part of the increasingly small minority that spoke Latin. Imagine going to church every week—some went every day—and having the sermon be delivered in a language you could not understand. This alienated the people from having a personal relationship with God and Christ and alienated them from the clergy and church.

In the early days of the Catholic Church, priests, bishops, and even popes were allowed to marry and father children. In the early 1100s, the church banned priests from getting married, insisting they remove themselves from "worldly desires" as much as possible. Priests were the most numerous and visible agents of the church, and this edict was enforced more on priests than it was on bishops or archbishops (many of whom came from rich, influential, or noble families), the College of

Cardinals in Rome (the body that administered church doctrine and law and advised the popes), and the pope himself.

All the way up the ladder of the Catholic hierarchy, officials had mistresses or women who were all but wives in name. Some also kept company with women "of ill repute." Many bishops, cardinals, and a number of popes had children.

This did not please many, but it was tolerated to a degree, depending on the country and time. What finally broke the Catholic Church's monopoly on religious beliefs was corruption. In the last chapter, we mentioned how Pope Leo X aided Christian II's conquest of Sweden. The pope loaned money to the Danish king to secure his power, which was not uncommon. However, Leo X was from the Medici family of Florence, who had risen from obscure wool traders outside Florence to arguably the richest family in all of Europe (the wealth of the Medici circa 1464 was equal to about 110 billion US dollars today). Florentine politics had forced Giovanni di Medici, who took the name "Leo X" on becoming pope, and his cousin Giulio, who became Pope Clement VII in 1523, into exile for some time. While these men were not poor by any means, they did not live according to their former standards while away from Florence. When Giovanni became Pope Leo X in 1513 and his cousin became a cardinal and papal advisor, the church entered into a period of corruption that had never been seen before.

Aside from Leo X's unbelievably lavish dinners that were the 16th-century equivalent of Hollywood's parties and galas today, he was a great collector and sponsor of art. He was responsible for commissioning Michelangelo's Sistine Chapel, among other famous projects. He also spread the wealth to his friends and supporters in other countries to influence events. No one is quite sure how much wealth Leo X spent, borrowed, and squandered, but it was a vast amount—so vast that it threatened to bankrupt the Catholic Church. And that's where a monk from the German town of Eisleben enters our story.

The immediate impetus to Martin Luther's rebellion against the Catholic Church was the sale of indulgences. An indulgence was essentially a "get-out-of-jail card" (in this case, jail was hell) for Catholics who felt they had sinned. An indulgence was simply a slip of paper that essentially forgave a certain sin for a price. So, if you commit a sin, you could just buy your way out of it. For minor sins, such as eyeing your neighbor's wife with lust, a smaller price was paid. If you needed a blanket indulgence for the past year, you would have to pay a higher price. If you were a noble, you would likely buy your way out of a number of sins for a higher price than a peasant. And the people believed this slip of paper would save their souls.

You might be wondering why. Most people still believed in both the infallibility of the church and its representatives. Since indulgences were approved by the pope, who was Christ's representative on Earth, most people believed in them. Making the con even worse was the fact that virtually none of the average people and many nobles could read Latin, so they had to take the clergy's word for it. Those in opposition to the sale of indulgences, such as Martin Luther, saw what was happening. The priests, monks, and other clergy who were selling indulgences were taking advantage of the poor and ignorant to line the coffers of the church and their own pockets. Charlatans even posed as clergy to make a quick buck.

Indulgences had existed for some time, but Leo X used them to full effect. Within a relatively short time, his coffers were being filled again, and since the mid-1400s, with the development of the printing press, the church could turn out indulgences in what would have been unimaginable numbers.

Indulgences were the main reason for Luther's rebellion against the church, but there were others. Luther knew of the corruptions plaguing the church, which included bribery, violence, and sexual abuse.

However, there were other more theological issues that Luther had issues with. One of them was the Catholic Church's monopoly on the

Bible and other holy works. In Luther's eyes, the people were subject to the interpretation of others; the clergy could twist the words of the Bible to suit their needs very easily. Luther also had issue with one of the bedrock principles of the church: that faith alone was enough to see one's soul into heaven. "Faith without works is dead" was one of the guiding principles of Luther's Reformation. It was not enough to simply say one had faith in God and Christ; one also had to show it. Most of the clergy (especially the parish priest, monks, and nuns) did do good works every day, but at the top, corruption and the disregard for the poor were ruining the church from within, at least according to Luther and others.

On All Hallows' Eve, Luther nailed what has become known as his *Ninety-five Theses* on the doors of the main church in Wittenberg, Germany. With that, the Protestant Reformation began. The *Ninety-five Theses* was a call for reform within the church, not a call for a break with it and the pope. But after Luther refused to renounce his statement, he was excommunicated (removed from the church, with the caveat that all Catholics shun or arrest him for heresy on sight).

Within a short time, Luther's ideas spread. He was supported by many disenchanted clergy in other parts of Europe, especially in the north. However, the ultimate success of the Reformation was dependent on European rulers who were willing to support the ideas with protection, money, and arms. The pope and many Catholic rulers were determined to stamp out the Reformation everywhere it presented itself. Of course, the violence was not one-sided. Many people now believed that Catholicism was completely corrupt and that they had been learning false lessons for generations. They used violence to attack their Catholic neighbors. (One of Luther's first deeds after his proclamation was to translate the Bible from Latin into German, something that was done in other areas, including Denmark. This allowed the ideas of Protestantism to spread more rapidly.) A century after Luther posted his *Ninety-five Theses*, the Thirty Years' War broke out; it was one of the costliest wars in European history.

How does this relate to Denmark? Well, no country, especially in the central and northern parts of Europe, where the ideas of the Reformation were strongest, was left untouched by the immense changes. Denmark experienced the beginnings of its Reformation in the early 1520s. While many of Luther's ideas seeped into Denmark between the time of his posting of the *Ninety-five Theses* and the 1520s, it was not until the Bible was translated into Danish in 1524 by linguists and philosophers Hans Mikkelsen and Christiern Vinter that the ideas of the Reformation became incredibly popular in Denmark.

Imagine a world where religion was the most important aspect of individual and social life for the vast majority of people. Then, imagine that the roots of that important aspect were hidden (in this case, behind Latin), so one had to take the word of the church as to both the Bible's contents and its interpretation. Once the Bible was translated into Danish and other languages, people could access the Word of God for themselves. They often did not like what they read, at least as far as the church's behavior was concerned.

One of the more immediate results of these translations was riots against Catholic churches and cathedrals on the grounds that Catholicism practiced idolatry, the worship of false idols. Christ preached against this practice in the New Testament. Idols included the elevation and portrayal of Mary (the mother of Christ), the Crucifixion, and the worship and veneration of relics, such as pieces of the True Cross, Christ's crown of thorns, and the bones of saints. Even the concept of sainthood began to be rejected since the elevation of a person to sainthood was dependent on the pope and possibly bribes paid to high church officials. Worst of all, at least for the Catholic Church, was the rejection of the pope as the representative of Christ on Earth.

The leading Danish reformer and theologian was Hans Tausen, who met and stayed with Martin Luther in Wittenberg for a year and a half. Luther was able to stay there because he had the protection of a local lord.

Illustration 8: Viborg Cathedral in central Denmark.
Naveen Kadri, CC BY-SA 3.0 <https://creativecommons.org/licenses/by-sa/3.0>, via Wikimedia Commons https://commons.wikimedia.org/w/index.php?curid=27494947

Tausen was a well-traveled man and had been to present-day Belgium and Holland, where he spoke to some of the early Humanist philosophers, who were developing ideas about the place of mankind in the universe separate from God (to a degree, as one had to be very careful at this time), human nature, and the future of human society. Tausen spoke not only Danish but also German, Latin, and Hebrew, which helped him immensely in both his translations and his subsequent orations on the ideas of the Reformation.

In 1525, Tausen was summoned back to his monastic order, which turned him out due to his refusal to reject the ideas of Luther and the Reformation, whose adherents had begun to be called Protestants–(those who protested against the church). He then moved to the Order of St. John in Viborg, where he delivered electrifying sermons to rapt audiences, some of whom traveled a day or more to hear him speak.

Eventually, however, even the relative patience that the Catholic Order of St. John had ran out. Tausen gave up his robes and went to the rulers of the city to ask for their protection, which was granted to him. For a time, he preached in the city's parish church, but eventually, so many people came to hear him that people were standing in the streets.

His next sermons took place in the city's marketplace, which was within earshot of not only those who wished to hear him but also those who did not. A proposal to allow Tausen to preach in the large church of the Franciscan Order was refused. Those supporting Tausen broke down the doors and surged in. With the situation about to turn seriously violent, an agreement was reached between Tausen and his supporters and the Catholic order. Within a short time, this compromise proved to be too much for the Catholic hierarchy. The local bishop summoned an armed crowd from the surrounding area and sent them to arrest Tausen and whatever followers they could lay their hands on. Because the situation was so tense, many of his followers had weapons with them, and the men sent to apprehend Tausen were turned back.

Illustration 9: Statue of Tausen at Ribe Cathedral today.

At this point, there were concerns that the violence would spread. The last Catholic king of Denmark, Frederick I, intervened and invited Tausen on a tour of the large port of Aalborg and made him one of his own chaplains. Though Frederick never renounced Catholicism, his openness was both criticized and lauded by the Danes, depending on their spiritual outlook. The king told Tausen to return to Viborg and give sermons. The people of the city were made responsible for his safety. One must remember that this was a time when even the most enlightened monarchs still used torture regularly, so this was a big step for Frederick to take. Denmark was still a majority Catholic nation, and any leaning toward Protestantism could affect both trade and Denmark's security. Frederick also had gone against his own oath, which stated that he would always be faithful to the church. Thus, doing this was a big risk.

Tausen began delivering his services only in Danish and began to create hymns and other worship songs in his native language. Sometime in the late 1520s, Tausen took an even further step away from Catholicism by marrying the sister of another reformer (his partner in creating Danish pamphlets about religion).

By this time, some of the Catholic orders in Viborg began to flee the city, and Tausen began to preach in the abandoned church of the Dominicans. Additionally, his standing-room-only sermons filled the Franciscan church, which the monks relinquished to him at the point of a spear carried by Frederick's soldiers and townspeople. It was only a matter of time, given the temper in Viborg and other Danish towns, before violence would flare up. This was happening not only in Denmark but also in much of northern and central Europe, including Norway and Sweden.

It was only a matter of time until Tausen began giving his sermons in Copenhagen (København in Danish), Denmark's beautiful capital. When he first arrived in Copenhagen in late 1529, Tausen was met with resistance from the city's bishop, who was accompanied by angry supporters. Fights ensued between Catholics and those who had followed Tausen to the city, as well as residents of Copenhagen who had read his pamphlets and were eager for him to speak. Though the Catholics prevented Tausen from speaking at the popular Church of St. Nicholas, Protestant crowds ran wild through the city, shouting insults at the church and the Catholic clergy. They ran into Catholic churches to destroy icons and paintings they deemed idolatrous.

The situation grew so serious, and the threat of civil war was so great (at least in the capital) that the Herrendag, the "Assembly of Nobles," met on July 2nd, 1530, to find some compromise between the two groups. Today, Tausen might be called a fanatic, as he did nothing to discourage the riots and demonstrations by his supporters while the assembly was meeting.

Over the next three years, this very tense situation remained in place until Frederick I died in April 1533. At that point, the Catholic hierarchy took matters into its own hands. They arrested Tausen, brought him before the Herrendag, and convicted him of blasphemy and expulsion from another parish where he had been speaking at the time. When the news was heard by the growing number of Protestants in the country, mob violence began in Copenhagen. The mob besieged the Herrendag and threatened to kill the clergy and nobles should Tausen not be released. This time, Tausen made the first move and calmed the crowd down. They escorted him to safety, and within a short time, the bishop in charge made an agreement with Tausen. He could preach safely as long as he toned the violent rhetoric. Tausen agreed.

In 1542, Tausen was made the bishop of Ribe (a Danish city), and he held that position for twenty years. Over those two decades, and with the help of his supporters and like-minded clergy throughout the country, Protestantism became the dominant Christian sect in Denmark, and it still is today. Most Danes do not attend church except for once a year for Christmas and maybe Easter, yet they do willingly pay a tax for the upkeep of the many medieval churches throughout the country.

Chapter 8 – Christian IV

There has been more than one queen of Denmark, but after Margaret I (r. 1387–1412) and until Margrethe II (r. 1972–present), Denmark's ruler was a man. Beginning with Christian II, the son of King Hans, in 1513, Danish kings have alternated in taking the names Christian and Frederick.

Many historians and Danes believe that the greatest Danish king was Christian IV, who ruled Denmark from 1588 to 1648. Though he was only eleven when he took the throne, his reign lasted sixty years, dying just shy of his seventy-first birthday.

Illustration 10: Contemporary etching of Christian IV (notice the hair braid) by Willem Delff. Courtesy Royal Collection Trust of the United Kingdom; *https://commons.wikimedia.org/wiki/File:Christian_IV._mit_Titel.jpg*

Christian was the son of Frederick II. Frederick had lost the Northern Seven Years' War (1563-1570) to Sweden, which means he failed in his attempt to restore Sweden to the Kalmar Union and lost some coastal territories to the Swedes. Frederick had also reformed the Danish tax system, which brought more money to the crown. This allowed him to rebuild the Danish Navy, which went on to defeat Scandinavian pirates. Frederick also improved the fortifications on the Sound (in Danish, Øresund), which controlled access into and out of the Baltic Sea. This, in turn, brought in more coins. By the time Frederick's son became king, Denmark was once again a prosperous nation. However, Frederick also had a cruel streak, which provides an interesting and very Gothic story.

In the aftermath of the mysterious death of the husband of Mary, Queen of Scots, in 1567, Frederick was asked to deliberate on the fate of James Hepburn, 4th Earl of Bothwell. He had been accused of taking part in the death of Henry Stuart, Lord Darnley, who was the husband of the queen. (Mary was believed by many to have played a part in her husband's death. Bothwell had gotten Mary pregnant with twins who were stillborn, though Mary later accused him of rape.) Bothwell and Mary fought a war against the many rebellious Scottish nobles, which went badly for the couple, who had aspirations to rule all of Britain. Mary surrendered, and Bothwell was "allowed" to escape to Scandinavia. This was a long journey, and he was eventually captured in Norway and brought to the Danish king.

Frederick had good relations with both England and Scotland, and he was asked to deliberate on Bothwell's fate to avoid disputes in Great Britain that might lead to war. Bothwell had been found guilty in Scotland, but it was up to Frederick to decide his punishment, which was exceedingly cruel. Bothwell was chained to a post in the dungeon of Dragsholm Castle, west of Copenhagen, in 1573. He died an insane man after having spent five unbelievably miserable years at the bottom of a Danish castle.

Though this cruel streak did not appear in Christian IV's personality, he was at times ruthless when he needed to be, such as when he ordered Danish troops into war with the Protestant German states in the Thirty Years' War against the wishes of his nobles in 1624. This ended poorly for Denmark, as it had to be rescued by its Swedish rivals (against whom Christian had lost in 1613) in order to prevent the loss of too much territory.

Christian had won victories over the Germans and had also proved himself in battle on land and sea in his youth. He even lost an eye in battle later in life. But his losses during the latter part of his reign cost him both his reputation and prestige, though, luckily for Christian and Denmark, he did not lose territory.

However, unlike most rulers in history who lost important wars and battles, Christian not only maintained his throne but also enjoyed popularity at home. The Danes best remember him for his popularity, as he began a series of changes that would echo down to the 20th century. He has been given the name "Renaissance King." The Renaissance is thought to have begun in Italy in the mid-1300s, so one would think there should have been a "Renaissance King" by the time Christian took the throne. The Renaissance came to Denmark and the rest of Scandinavia in the 1400s, long before Christian IV came to the throne. But certain things happened during his reign that make him stand out.

First, there was a reflowering of ancient thought in Denmark during the Renaissance. This was helped immensely by the invention of the printing press in nearby Germany around 1450. However, the many wars with neighboring Sweden and the Hansa cost the Danish Crown much treasure. Their money was spent on defenses and keeping kings in power, which means their wealth was not spent on the patronage of the arts, letters, and sciences. Also, though there were, of course, painters and sculptors in the Renaissance period in Denmark, the greatest period of Danish visual art would come in the latter part of the 1800s and early 20th century. For instance, the famous statue, *The Little Mermaid*, by Edvard Eriksen (1876-1959), was created during this time; it stands in Copenhagen today. The same was true for the written word. The world knows the name and works of Hans Christian Andersen (1805-1875), who wrote "The Little Mermaid," and Karen Blixen (1885-1962), who is best known for the famous autobiography *Out of Africa* and many short stories. The famous philosopher Søren Kierkegaard (1813-1855) was also a Dane.

Illustration 11: The Little Mermaid in Copenhagen.

In the visual realm, the greatest impact the Renaissance had on Denmark was in the many churches and cathedrals that were built or rebuilt. Two prime examples of this are Roskilde Cathedral and Kronborg Castle.

Illustration 12: Roskilde Cathedral
CucombreLibre from New York, NY, USA, CC BY 2.0
<https://creativecommons.org/licenses/by/2.0>, via Wikimedia Commons
https://commons.wikimedia.org/wiki/File:Roskilde_Cathedral_aerial.jpg

Another factor affecting the arrival and influence of the Renaissance in Denmark was the establishment of Protestantism. The Catholic Church encouraged the expression of the visual arts during the Renaissance period with religious works, such as Michelangelo's famous Sistine Chapel and *The Last Judgment*). This encouragement bled into other areas, such as portraiture and ancient and mythological themes. However, one aspect of the Reformation was the rejection of what many saw as idols. The rejection of any likeness of a person or the divine had an immediate dampening effect on the spread of the visual arts in not only Denmark but also Norway and Sweden. After Martin Luther, other more militant reformers arose, most notably John Calvin in Switzerland. Calvinism was a more extreme branch of Protestantism, and while it was rejected by the mainstream Protestant Church in Denmark, many Scandinavians embraced the stoic, grim, fatalistic, and determined sect. Many have called Calvinism a "joyless" sect. Although this is an overstatement, the advancement of Protestantism, with its frowning outlook on artistic expression, prevented the visual arts from fully blooming in Denmark and elsewhere in northern Europe for at least a century and a half, if not more.

So, why was Christian IV called the "Renaissance King?" "Renaissance" means "rebirth," and in much of Europe, this "rebirth" had to do with the arts and letters. So, although Christian suffered defeats in war and died a somewhat bitter man, he reformed and restructured the Danish economy, reformed aspects of its society, and built (and rebuilt) universities, churches, and public buildings throughout Denmark. He provided both scholarships and loans to students personally. He also founded new castles and palaces, some of which were at the cutting edge at the time. "Renaissance King" also alludes to the fact that, at heart, Christian was a "Renaissance man," as he valued learning and had many interests.

Christian even founded entire towns and cities, the most famous of which was Kristiania, better known as Oslo today, the capital of modern Norway. Though he commissioned the establishment of various cities, he also took part in the design and layout of some of the towns named for him. The port of Christianshavn (*havn* meaning harbor in Danish) in Denmark, which has been subsumed by the growth of Copenhagen, and Kristiansand in western Norway were established by and named for him, as were Kristianstad and Kristianopel in Sweden.

Personally, Christian was loved by most of his people, though his son-in-law did lead a rebellion of nobles that resulted in the diminishment of his power. He was seen as a Falstaff-like character to many. He was larger than life, a lover of beer, a prankster with a joke at the ready, and a man of action. Christian also studied Latin and theology, grilling prospective candidates for the upper clergy for their knowledge of Scripture, theology, and Christian history. He developed new types of guns and undertook to test them himself for both safety and effectiveness. He was also a truly able sea captain and had taken part in a few sea battles as a young man. He joined his admirals and shipbuilders in designing and testing his warships.

Christian lost money, men, and prestige due to his military defeats, though luckily for both Denmark and the king himself, by and large, Danish lands were not lost. The reestablishment of Danish rule in the now German state of Schleswig-Holstein was also a result of Christian's rule. Denmark, as a nation, took a giant step forward during Christian's reign due to his efforts or to the weakening of monarchical power, which evolved in the 19th and 20th centuries to become a fully-fledged constitutional monarchy.

Sadly for Christian, he died an unhappy man at the age of seventy in 1648. He had been born into a warrior family, so he was extremely disappointed that his efforts to grow Danish influence, power, and territory came to naught.

Chapter 9 – Danish Life and Changes in It, From Top to Bottom (1700–1814)

In 1647, Christian IV's eldest son, who was also named Christian, fell ill and died. In 1658, Christian IV's eldest surviving son, Frederick III, who had become king in 1648 after his father's death, signed the Treaty of Roskilde, ending the Second Northern War with Sweden. This defeat cost the Danes their remaining holdings in southern Sweden and two valuable provinces in Norway. They also lost the island of Bornholm in the southeast of the tip of the Swedish peninsula. This was a valuable fortress and fishing and agricultural area. While the Danes eventually regained the island (it is still Danish today), the end of the Second Northern War essentially marked out the European territories Denmark holds today. At this time, Iceland was Danish (it gained independence in 1944), as was Greenland (it is still officially part of Denmark but has a great deal of autonomy) and the Faroe Islands, which is halfway between Scotland and Iceland (it is an autonomous territory today).

Illustration 13: Frederick III in 1656 by Karel van Mander.
https://commons.wikimedia.org/wiki/File:Frederik_III_i_rustning.jpg

Though Denmark would take part in wars after 1658, for the most part, the conflicts were few. Successive Danish governments since then have largely concentrated on peaceful pursuits. Repeated defeats by Sweden from the mid-1500s and then the rise of Prussia in northern Europe and its subsequent leadership in uniting the German states as one nation (1864–1871) meant that, in population, riches, and territory, Denmark was no longer able to initiate wars as it had previously. One glaring exception exists in 1864, which we will talk about in Chapter 11. (As a side note, by the mid to late 1600s, Sweden had risen to be a great power in European affairs. It was supported by an excellent military and had kings who were ahead of their time strategically, tactically, and politically. This ended with the Swedish loss at Poltava in Ukraine to the Russians under Peter the Great in 1709.)

Christian IV's defeats and efforts to concentrate more power in the hands of the monarch at the expense of the nobility caused a backlash. The nobles of Denmark wrested a considerable amount of power back from the monarchy by the end of Christian's life in 1648. Under Frederick III, who inherited his father's dislike of the nobility, major changes would occur in the structure of the Danish upper classes and the people.

While the Danes naturally played a political (and, to an extent, military role in northern Europe from 1658 onward and built strong defenses to prevent attacks, the focus of the monarch, the nobles, and the people gradually turned inward.

To a large degree, Frederick blamed the nobility for the defeats against Sweden during both his and his father's reign. The nobles filled the officer class and were his top commanders. To a degree, "donations" that financed the war came from the nobility, although they may have been coerced in one way or another to donate. The nobility had been exempted from taxes for some time.

In the 1400s, there were around 250 noble families in Denmark. Christian IV took measures to strip many nobles of their rank, and by 1640, the number of noble families had been reduced to 140. As you can see, there were many reasons why the nobles wished to wrest political power from Christian during his reign, which was successful to a large degree.

Frederick was determined to regain the power his father had lost. He used threats, promises, and the prestige of his position to gain support for a decree in which he pronounced the monarchy "hereditary for all time." This means that the king or queen had to be one of his descendants. This not only guaranteed the title for his lineage, but it also meant that Frederick would rule as an absolute monarch, as would his future children, grandchildren, etc. Shortly thereafter, the Danish nobles were stripped of most of their tax exemptions. One of their remaining exemptions, paying tax on their land, was removed by Frederick's son Christian V (r. 1670–1699) in 1688.

Another one of Frederick III's reforms was his opening of the bureaucracy to "commoners." These men (and they were only men) were "common" in the sense that they were not of the nobility, but they were not small landholding farmers or shoemakers. These "commoners" were of the growing middle class who lived in the cities of Denmark. Today, the majority of these men would be considered upper class or even part of the "1 percent," but at the time, in virtually all European countries, the middle class was very small. These were men of wealth who did not hold titles. Frederick's reform was a revolutionary change in Danish affairs, considering the centuries of traditions and laws broken by this action, and set the nation on the path that resulted in the amazingly egalitarian Denmark of today.

These middle-class bureaucrats would come to head the king's "colleges" (in this case, a synonym for "government department") of commerce, war, the navy, and finance. They would administer these areas for the king and would also serve as an advisory cabinet to the monarch. These men helped devise a new tax system that would take Denmark into the 1800s, and they worked with the king to promulgate a written, formal nationwide law code. Elements of this code took power or at least prerogatives out of the hands of the nobles.

One of the many results that came from adding men of ability rather than birth to the government infrastructure was Denmark's defenses were strengthened. Though Denmark's time of offensive warfare was over, it was still surrounded by nations that had proven themselves hostile many times in the past. From the early 1600s through the early to middle part of the 1700s, Sweden's search for power, riches, and influence brought it into conflict with Denmark. Now that the Danes had lost southern Sweden to the Swedes, there was very little preventing the Swedes from attacking Denmark directly. So, the Danes built a growing series of fortifications on its coastline and southern borders in the area of today's Germany. At the same time, the Danes also spent much money modernizing their navy, which, along with the forts lining the Sound, would ensure Denmark controlled access from the Baltic to the North Sea and out into the Atlantic.

Illustration 14: Sofia Magdalena by Carl Gustaf Pilo.
https://commons.wikimedia.org/w/index.php?curid=52113251

In 1780, under Frederick III's 3x descendant Christian VII, Denmark signed a neutrality agreement with Russia, the Netherlands, and Sweden. The Swedes were the main concern, but in 1766, Swedish King Gustav III married Danish Crown Princess Sofia Magdalena. It was an unhappy marriage, but it went a long way to establishing peaceful relations with the two former enemies.

Before we move on to the changes within Denmark itself, we should at least mention Denmark's empire in the Western Hemisphere. The Danes acquired the islands of St. Thomas, St. John, and St. Croix in 1672, 1718, and 1733, respectively. (Today, these islands are known as the US Virgin Islands, which were bought from Denmark in 1917 during WWI.) These islands, especially St. Croix, were rich in sugar, a commodity that was in high demand. To grow, harvest, and package this and other crops, Denmark, like the other European nations with colonies in the New World, used slaves. By 1740, about 90 percent of St. Croix's population was enslaved people.

During Viking times, the raiders seized slaves from every area they raided and sold them in their and other territories. A large number of these people were Irish, but many were from today's England and France. The Danes also sold or bought enslaved people from the Swedes, who raided and traded in the Baltic states, Poland, Russia, and Ukraine. It was exceedingly rare for the Vikings to have slaves from the Middle East or Africa in Scandinavia, but considering the contact they had with the Byzantine Empire, which sat between Europe, Asia, and Africa, it would not have been impossible.

However, as the Europeans moved farther down the African coast, the slave trade between that continent and the Western Hemisphere increased. The Danes traded in people via the Danish East India Company, but the enslaved African population became nearly self-sustaining by the late 1700s.

In 1792, the Danes made slavery in Denmark illegal, though it continued in the Virgin Islands until slave rebellions in 1848 resulted in their emancipation. However, the Danish East India Company merely switched its route and became a minor but significant part of the slave trade from Africa to the American colonies.

One sadly ironic part of this stain on Denmark's history was that as the nation increased its participation in the slave trade, with all of its pain and misery, events and people at home were taking steps to move toward a freer society, one that would lay the groundwork of one of today's most free, happy, and economically satisfied nations.

Though slavery did not exist in Denmark after 1792, the country had long been based on blood and nobility. For most people, especially those in the countryside, which would make up the majority of the population until the late 1800s, they were often tied to a specific area or noble for their entire lives or the majority of it. Peasants were not allowed to leave the land of their birth unless they had permission from the local noble, and it was not unusual for peasants to be "lent" to friends or permanently given to them as a type of non-monetary trade. Peasants were rarely given away like this as Denmark moved into the modern era of the 1700s, but life as a peasant was still not an easy one.

Throughout most of Danish history, especially after the establishment of feudalism in the 11th and 12th centuries, peasants were subject to corvée, which required them to work the lands of the nobility. They also often had to pay a percentage of their own crops. It was not until the reforms of the late 1700s that most Danish farmers were given the legal right to own their own land.

In the 1720s, the nobility attempted to increase the amount of time required by the corvée to three days a week from two. At the time, fewer than three hundred noble families owned 90 percent of the land. They had a workforce that was just one step up from slavery that cost them nothing to utilize. The nobles had immense power over the peasantry for much of Denmark's history.'

Illustration 15: Many modern Danish small landholding farms look much as they did from the later 1700s onward. This is a typical farm, but it was owned by the famous Danish author Isak Dinesen, which was the pen name for Karen Blixen, the subject of the film Out of Africa.

Male peasants were required to spend forty years working the land of their lord, though they were able to commute this to six years if they served in the military. The problem was the nobles decided which of the peasants on their land could serve. Not only did this give the aristocracy great power over the lives of the peasants, but it also gave them considerable negotiating power with the king. Unless the king hired mercenaries, which was expensive but often done, he was dependent on the nobility's willingness to raise an army for him. If the king was strong, they were very willing. The same could not be said about weak kings, though. For those kings who were not very powerful or merely a figurehead, negotiations would have to take place in order for the king to raise an army. This would result in an incredibly Byzantine series of favors and negotiations that weakened the king or the nobility, depending on the current state of affairs and the negotiating skill of those involved.

On a more local level, nobles were essentially *the* law in their domain. A peasant could not testify against them in court, and the nobles were allowed to inflict corporal punishment, which included beatings, whipping, the stocks, and more, on peasants they found "breaking the law." As you might imagine, sexual predation was rife, with women and girls outside of the aristocracy virtually without any legal recourse from being assaulted. It is important to note that these situations were not unique to just Denmark, although they are terrible to think about.

From the early decades of the 18th century to the rise of Napoleon Bonaparte, Europe and the brand-new United States went through an amazing period known as the Enlightenment. Those who live in Western-style democracies today can thank the men and women of the Enlightenment for the idea that people are endowed with certain rights, such as those of speech, movement, and redress from the government. These people opened the way for those today to have a say in the rules and laws under which they live instead of the often-arbitrary wishes and desires of some noble or king. The Enlightenment is one of the most fascinating periods of human history, but we don't have much time to dwell on it in this particular book. Suffice it to say that, for our purposes here, Enlightenment thoughts, coupled with the desire for greater profits, spurred great changes in Denmark, Europe, and North America in the 1700s and onward to today. Oftentimes, people think about the freedoms that are enjoyed in the West in a political way, and without a doubt, new and different political changes began to occur in Denmark in the 1700s. These changes were not the temporary changes that had been made throughout Danish history in regard to who would have power in the country. Rather, they involved the way Danes lived and worked. The 18th century marked a turning point that truly laid the foundations of Danish society today, from top to bottom. Denmark was no different in this than other western European countries (with the exceptions of Portugal, Spain, and many of the states of Italy). These countries were all making advances in agriculture and industry, beginning what would become known as the Industrial Revolution.

Though it may sound odd at first, what spurred many of Denmark's economic gains was the legalization of the free press in 1770. With the opening of a public forum where the issues of the day could be discussed and debated, new developments in farming technology and techniques began to spread. (Denmark opened its educational system to all Danes in 1814, and for the time, Denmark was a relatively literate society, especially in the cities and especially in Copenhagen.)

Changes that large could not simply arrive without affecting other parts of life. One of the hindrances to more modern farming practices was the poor land records and boundaries resulting from the inefficient central administration and unrecorded land exchanges between nobles over the years. This caused disputes between nobles, leading to the rise of "common land," which traditionally was worked for the peasants for themselves. The land owned or used by those other than the nobility in the first part of the 18th century was only about 10 percent, and a large portion of this was owned by the Protestant Church.

The other problem was more personal to most Danes than nobles' land boundaries. This was, of course, the corvée. The corvée required peasants to work their noble's land for a proscribed number of days per week. Since the peasants had little incentive to work under the corvée, output remained low, and new methods were not sought.

In 1759, the system of enclosure, which fenced in and formally drew boundaries, was enacted. There was very little resistance to this move, unlike in England. Enclosure made clear farm boundaries, eliminated many legal and personal conflicts, and resulted in the establishment of the Royal Danish Agricultural Society in 1769. This society supported and encouraged new developments in farming and farming technologies. Enclosure also opened up, both by design and accident, many of the lands outside of the reach of the nobility and clergy, and a growing number of Danish farms were created over the course of the next decades. The nobles were compensated for losses, and a number of fairly large farm holdings, which were run by the growing middle class, sprang into existence. (There are farms and ranches in the United States and Australia that are larger than the entire country of Denmark, so "large" is a relative term.) The number of small landholding family farms increased as well. But although many reforms were enacted in the 18th to the mid-19th century, small peasant farms were still subjected to a large number of restrictions.

During the 1760s, the corvée was reformed, allowing farmers to concentrate on their own subsistence farms or seek work with someone other than their lord. Though it does not seem "modern" today, this change, which allowed farmers to pay a fee rather than work the land, gave farmers more time. This, in turn, incentivized labor, which contributed to a rise in production never before seen in Denmark. Many of these changes were implemented in Norway (which, at the time, was still a Danish territory), though the land in Norway was (and still is) less productive than Denmark.

From 1784 to 1788, the Great Agricultural Commission of Denmark, which was formed by order of King Christian VII (r. 1766–1808), studied agriculture in Denmark and made recommendations for reforms. The growing power and numbers of the middle and lower classes made this reform urgent and also welcome. From the peasants' point of view, the most welcome reform was the elimination of the laws tying a peasant to the land of their birth. To help create new farms, the government would issue low-interest loans to purchase the land.

Chapter 10 – Napoleon and the Aftermath of the Napoleonic Wars

Ever since the end of the Second Northern War in 1720, Denmark had felt peace. The French Revolution and the turbulence it caused was felt in Denmark, as it was in most of Europe, but the nation managed to remain relatively untouched by the domestic tumult caused by the ideas of the French Revolution.

Some of the ideas of the French Revolution did spread into Denmark and ultimately affected change within the country, but the Danish monarchy was relatively unaffected. When the French Revolution began in 1789, the king of Denmark was Christian VII. His son, Frederick VI, was conservative and strongly protected the rights and prerogatives of the monarchy. Though he was popular at first, Frederick ended his reign as a defeated and increasingly out-of-touch king. The reason for this decline was simple: Napoleon Bonaparte.

Illustration 16: Frederick VI in a portrait from early in his reign by Friedrich Carl Gröger
https://commons.wikimedia.org/wiki/File:Fiedrichvidenmark.jpg

Denmark's location has been both a positive and a negative throughout its history. As you know by now, it was situated between the North and Baltic Seas, which provided it with both power and coin. Throughout most of its history, Denmark managed to control the straits and sounds knifing through and around the country, allowing Denmark to become one of the region's greatest powers for centuries.

However, by 1800, Denmark's position near France brought it into possible conflict with its leader, Napoleon, due to its renown as a regional sea power. Napoleon Bonaparte had gained more and more power after his takeover of the French government in 1799. In 1794, both Denmark and Sweden declared themselves neutral in the conflicts that were taking place in Europe. In 1800, as a result of Napoleon's pressure, both Russia and the powerful German state of Prussia joined this neutrality pact.

There was one problem with this pact: Britain, France's greatest foe, was not "neutral" at all. Strictly speaking, these neutral countries said they would trade with anyone, but the reality was most of their trade (including the resources needed to make war) was with France. When Napoleon came to power in his own right, he created the Continental System, which forbade any European power from trading with Great Britain. (The success and failure of this system have filled volumes; suffice it to say that it was only partially successful for a variety of reasons, one of them being the wealth and naval power of Britain.)

Adhering to this system brought Denmark into conflict with Britain, and in 1800, the British Royal Navy sought to end the use of the Danish fleet as a go-between in France's trade in the Baltic. The British attacked and destroyed most of the Danish fleet in Copenhagen Harbor. Like many of the nations affected by the Continental System, the Danes went on to trade with Napoleon, but they increasingly entered into secret agreements with the British, something that continued until 1807.

By 1807, the remnants of the Danish fleet had been augmented by new ships. While this fleet was not as powerful as it had been, the British feared that it could be used by Napoleon. The French Navy had been almost completely destroyed by the British Royal Navy under the famous Admiral Horatio Nelson at Trafalgar in 1805, and despite having been weakened considerably at sea, it was not out of the realm of possibility that Napoleon might use Danish ships as part of a French invasion of Great Britain. This possibility, which the British thought they had prevented with their victory at Trafalgar, reared its head again when Napoleon and Russian Tsar Alexander I (r. 1801–1825) signed a treaty of friendship at Tilsit (now located in the Russian Baltic enclave of Kaliningrad). This caused the British to fear that Napoleon might once again focus on invading England, as his eastern flank was now protected.

In response to this and to take control of the entrance to the North Sea itself, the British attacked Denmark in August 1807, occupying the island of Zealand, the location of the Danish capital of

Copenhagen. The city was subjected to a ruthless bombardment, which set fire to parts of the city and killed hundreds, if not thousands. Seventy-five percent of the city was destroyed, and the Danes were forced to accede to British demands, which included the seizure of the Danish fleet.

Illustration 17: The Terrible Bombardment of Copenhagen by Christoffer Wilhelm Eckersberg "Father of Danish painting"), c. 1807

https://commons.wikimedia.org/wiki/File:Copenhagen_on_fire_1807_by_CW_Eckersberg.jpg

Naturally, this drove the Danes into the waiting arms of Napoleon, who, despite his loss at Trafalgar, was at the height of his power in Europe. On Halloween 1807, the Danes joined Napoleon against the British. Once again, the Royal Navy returned, this time imposing a blockade on Denmark. One of the most significant aspects of this blockade was that important shipments of grain (both Danish and European) to Norway were curtailed. Norway nearly reached famine-like proportions. Even the relaxation of the blockade in 1810 did not wipe out the hunger in Norway. It convinced many there that independence was the future. (Norway became part of Sweden in 1815 as a result of the Concert of Europe, which redrew the map of Europe after the defeat of Bonaparte, but it gained its independence in 1905.)

By 1813, the tide had turned against Napoleon. In 1812, he turned on and was then defeated by the Russians. He was forced to retreat with an ever-dwindling number of starving, disease-ridden troops back to France. Nation after nation turned against him, including Sweden. However, Denmark did not. Its weakened state and size, combined with a hatred of Britain for the destruction of Copenhagen, meant that the Danes remained Napoleon's allies.

The Swedes had become allies of the British in 1813 and declared war on the Danes shortly thereafter. (Ironically, Sweden was ruled by King Karl XIV Johan (or Charles XIV John), the founder of today's Swedish royal family. He was actually the former French Marshal Jean-Baptiste Bernadotte, a noted general in Napoleon's army and the husband of a former fiancée to the French emperor. He had been chosen by the Swedes as their new monarch in 1809 after a revolution against their former king.). The Swedes surprised the Danes by invading the country from the south. The Treaty of Kiel in January 1814 saw Denmark relinquish Norway to the Swedes. A Norwegian rebellion led by the heir to the Danish throne, the future Christian VIII, who was the governor, was met with defeat.

Denmark's relationship with Napoleon had been a disaster. Europe's greatest powers had either opposed or turned on the French at some point, but Denmark remained tied to France until the end. Both political and economic relationships were soured for years. Copenhagen had to essentially be rebuilt (though, for us in the 21st century, this was a blessing, as the rebuilding of Copenhagen, which lasted through the rest of the 19th century, resulted in one of Europe's most beautiful cities). Denmark's economy was also in shambles, and to make economic matters even worse, the British imposed extremely high duties on Danish grain, a move that other nations followed. Farmers, both rich and poor, had to sell their lands, and many nobles were forced to sell estates that had been in their families for perhaps hundreds of years. All of the reforms that had begun in the 1700s were brought to a standstill.

Most of Denmark's overseas trade was taken over by the independent German city of Hamburg. Inflation made life almost impossible. In 1813, just before the first defeat of Napoleon (he would come back in his famous "Hundred Days" to rebuild his army, only to be defeated at Waterloo), Denmark declared bankruptcy.

From 1813 to 1818, Denmark suffered from economic depression and uncertainty. In 1818, however, the establishment of an independent national bank led to the economy's recovery and kept the treasury out of the hands of the king and his advisors. Denmark slowly moved out of the worst depression in its memory. By 1830, the economy had recovered. Prices were stable, the land reforms of the 1700s were starting to take real effect, and Danish overseas trade began to make a comeback.

Frederick VI, who had once been popular, remained in power, but he held on to conservative principles and refused to consider the new economic and political ideas that had come to Europe via the Industrial and French Revolutions. His advisors were all conservative nobles, and what changes were wrought were often a result of long protracted debates with the king and his close advisors.

Things began to change in 1830 when a wave of revolutionary protests swept western Europe. These people opposed many of the conservative policies that followed after the defeat of the French. They brought up the revolutionary ideas France had initially fought for. In Denmark, this forced the king to allow the formation of national and regional assemblies, whose role was to advise and consult with the king. Unfortunately, most of these assemblies did not have the right to make or pass laws. Over the next two decades, change happened in Denmark, but it happened slowly. One of the ways the urban middle class and sometimes the farmers made themselves known was in the independent liberal newspapers, which began to rise in number. These newspapers excoriated the king and the nobility for being unwilling to enact reforms that most of the country was calling for.

Frederick VI died in 1839, and his cousin, who became King Christian VIII, took the throne. He was thought to be more liberal in his views than his uncle. However, by the time Christian took the throne, he had grown more conservative and believed that change was happening too quickly. He believed (and he may have been correct) that Denmark needed time to absorb the changes, which had been increasing in speed since the late 1700s. Christian concentrated his efforts on developing an efficient government and administration. These reforms gave more power to local governments, and, partially through them, more and more liberal policies were experimented with and refined.

A momentous change was to come in the 1840s. One reason for this was the rise of the farming class in what has become known in Denmark as the Farmers' Movement. Originally, the movement was more of a religious revival, but as time went by, farmers began to call for additional reforms, with representation in government being the most consequential.

Christian VIII died in January 1848. The brevity of his reign, which was only nine years, was unusual, for many of his predecessors since the late 1600s had ruled for decades. His death, though, could not have come at a better time for Denmark. Christian's death, combined with a new wave of revolution in 1848 (with many of the disturbances occurring to Denmark's immediate south in the many states of what was to become Germany), led to the beginning of a new age in Denmark.

The new king, Frederick VII, appointed a cabinet that included the liberals Orla Lehmann and Ditlev Monrad, who were both sons of middle-class families. Both of them would hold important positions in the government and lead the new National Liberal Party. On June 5th,

1849, Denmark had a new constitution, one that eliminated the absolute monarchy and replaced it with a constitutional monarchy, similar to Britain's. The king and his cabinet were balanced by two new representative bodies, which were similar to those in Britain. The Folketing was the Danish version of the House of Commons, and the Landsting resembled the House of Lords. An independent judiciary was created, which protected the rights now enshrined in the new constitution: free press, free speech, the right to assemble, and religious freedom. Last but not least, the vote was given to all adult men, regardless of class, which was a monumental shift in how the country ran. (Women were given the vote in 1915.) Today, the Danish government consists of a unicameral assembly (the Folketing), with a prime minister as the head of government.

The second half of the 19th century would prove to be momentous for Denmark. While the nation sustained a humiliating defeat in a war against Prussia and Austria in 1864, its economic trajectory was mostly upward, helped by the great changes taking place throughout Europe and North America. Railways were built throughout the small nation, facilitating trade with Europe by land, and the many harbors of the country were modernized. The Danish shipping industry grew by leaps and bounds, and the importation of coal and iron from Germany fueled new industries. Farming production increased, and Danish bacon and butter, which today are both highly prized commodities among restaurants and foodies, became world-renowned.

The changes in the government protected the individual to some extent, but economically, many Danish workers were at the mercy of ownership. Like many other nations in Europe, especially in the west, Danish workers in many industries began to form labor unions and trade cooperatives. While there was some resistance to these developments among the upper and upper-middle classes, it did not resemble the intense opposition to unionization found in other industrial countries, especially the United States. In the last quarter of the 19th century and into the first decade and a half of the 20th century, the Danish economy enjoyed virtually uninterrupted advancement.

Chapter 11 – The Second Schleswig-Holstein War

The two southernmost provinces of Denmark in 1864 were Schleswig and Holstein. Due to an agreement many centuries prior, Danish kings also carried the title duke of Schleswig and Holstein. At times, due to negotiation, war, or both, the king was only the duke of one or the other. For a time, both provinces were controlled by German princes/dukes, and they were part of the Holy Roman Empire. When they were Danish, the king/duke ruled them as his personal property. The reforms of the 1800s were, of course, felt, but ultimately, the king ruled one or both provinces as an absolute ruler. Today, the former duchies of Schleswig and Holstein are combined into one German state: Schleswig-Holstein. Schleswig is the northernmost of the two.

What became known as the "Schleswig-Holstein Question" was complicated, as it involved ethnic identity, royal power, the wave of nationalism (which had arisen in 1848 and had not abated), and the rising power of Prussia. Prussia, under its chancellor, Otto von Bismarck, was in the beginning stages of creating a new nation, Germany, with the Prussian monarch at its head.

Following the French Revolution and the revolutions of 1848, the people of Europe began to think of themselves as nations of people (usually people of the same ethnic and linguistic group, generally speaking) rather than subjects of a king or queen. For these nationalists, a nation was only complete when all of its ethnic relations were within the same borders. In Holstein, the majority of the population was German. In Schleswig, the majority was Danish, though there was a substantial German population.

Making things more complicated was the fact that, when the Congress of Europe met to settle the borders of Europe in 1815 after the fall of Bonaparte, Holstein was included in the German Confederation and subject to its laws, although it was still the personal property of the Danish king. As the 19th century continued, more and more people in Holstein wanted closer ties with Germany and an end to its role as the Danish king's backyard.

In Schleswig, the German population, which was a more liberally minded group of people for the time, wished to end its role as part of Denmark's personal holdings and its union or affiliation with Holstein and the German Confederation. This clashed with feelings of nationalism in Denmark, which only increased as more power was shared with the people. Germans in both duchies rebelled in 1849, and a low-level insurgency continued until 1851, when, despite receiving aid from Prussia, the rebels were defeated. This was known as the First Schleswig War.

Though the Danes were victorious, the great powers of Europe (Britain, France, and Austria-Hungary) forced the Danes to agree that Denmark would not annex Schleswig or tie it to Denmark any more than the majority-German Holstein was. However, the two duchies still belonged to the Danish king, and none of the reforms passed in 1849 had any effect on either of the two territories. The terms of the peace, known as the London Protocol of 1852, stated that the people of Holstein would be subject to the same constitutional changes as the rest of Denmark. In 1863, the new king, Christian IX, who was not Prussia's preferred choice, declared that all of Denmark's laws would be enforced in Holstein as well, something that virtually none of the people of Holstein wanted. On top of that, it was a violation of the London Protocol.

This last point gave Prussian Chancellor Bismarck the opening he was looking for. He realized that the situation in Schleswig and Holstein was the perfect opportunity to neutralize any possible moves Denmark might make to prevent the unification of Germany. More importantly, it would stymie the plans of Prussia's rival (and ally in 1864), Austria-Hungary.

In 1864, Austria-Hungary was still a power to be reckoned with, but it was not the world power it had been. Still, the Austro-Hungarian emperor and state still had immense influence in the German states, some of which were actually Austrian properties. If Prussia couldn't remove Austrian influence in the smaller states of Germany, it would never be able to unite them under its own banner.

Strangely enough, in order to weaken Austria-Hungary and create a pretext for war against it, Bismarck needed to defeat Denmark. Denmark had violated the terms of the London Protocol and attempted to basically annex Holstein, which gave Bismarck the excuse he needed. The Austrians were the power behind many of the northern German states, and it could not afford to have Denmark or Prussia gain influence in the area. In order to keep itself a player in the area, Austria allied itself with Prussia, and the Second Schleswig War began on February 1st, 1864.

The war lasted until October, but by the time a formal peace treaty had been signed, the Danes had been long defeated on the battlefield. The armed forces of Prussia and Austria separately were too much for the Danes. And when combined, Denmark did not have a chance, though it attempted to create a defensive line along the ancient Danevirke (Danework).

This defensive system had a number of flaws. First, it had not been kept in good condition, especially since the 1700s, when Denmark enjoyed a long period of peace. The Danework in 1864 was a series of trenchworks and high berms, and it was no match for the modern weapons of the Prussians and Austrians. What's more, these fortifications did not run across the whole of the southern part of Jutland; they ended on marshy land in the east, which was believed to be impassible by large forces. You can probably guess what happened: the Prussians flanked the bulk of the Danish forces by going through the marshes.

The Treaty of Vienna (1864) stipulated that Prussia would administer Schleswig and that Holstein would be administered by Austria-Hungary. Bismarck was aware that a problem would likely arise, as Prussians would need to pass through Austrian-controlled territory to administer and trade with Schleswig, and he was correct. Adding fuel to the fire was the fact that a delegation from Schleswig attended meetings of the German Confederation, which was dominated by Austria, despite being forbidden to. Prussia accused Austria of attempting to annex Schleswig, and both sides began to mobilize troops. The resultant Austro-Prussian War was the second phase of Bismarck's plan to unify Germany under the Prussian royal family. The defeat of France in 1871 in the Franco-Prussian War was the final step, and in 1871, Germany as we know it was created.

At the end of WWII, the boundaries of the country were drawn again. Rather than push for both Schleswig and Holstein to be given to Denmark, the Danes asserted that the northern part of Schleswig should be given back since it was majority Danish. The borders of Denmark have been the same since.

For the Danes, the defeat of 1864 was truly the end of Denmark's role as any kind of substantial power in Europe. Since that time, the Danes have not been involved in any major way in any world conflict, though the nation was overrun by Hitler's Germany on April 9th, 1940.

Chapter 12 – The Twentieth Century to WWII

At the beginning of the 20th century, Denmark was a much different nation than it had been at the start of the 19th century. Tremendous reforms had taken place throughout the 1800s that resulted in a nation that was more equitable and freer in 1901. Though the old aristocratic families still enjoyed some privileges and status (after all, thousands of years of law and tradition do not simply disappear overnight), the legal and cultural playing field was being leveled. Although there was some overlap, the nobility was no longer the only class with influence and power, as the new industrial class was taking over. Something similar happened in much of western Europe.

Luckily for Denmark, many in the rising class of industrialists had been raised at a time when liberalism was the order of the day. In 1901, the conservatives, who tended to back a stronger monarchy, saw the writing on the wall vis-à-vis the king. They came to an agreement with their liberal colleagues in the Folketing, which asserted that the king's role was to appoint the government from the assembly, not from his inner circle or the nobility. This custom was only enshrined into law in 1953, though it had been honored for fifty-two years.

Over the course of the first decades of the 20th century, Denmark began on the path that has resulted in its population being one of the happiest and most satisfied nations on Earth today. Education reforms opened the doors to virtually all Danes, and entry into Denmark's large number of universities became easier for the lower economic class. Tax reforms increased the state's coffers, and many loopholes were closed.

Lastly, free trade measures were put into place. This meant that many tariffs on imported goods were removed, giving Danes more choices and improving, for the most part, international relations. In return, many European nations lowered their barriers to Danish goods, which benefited both sides.

However, as you likely know, the early part of the 20th century was a time of great anxiety. Germany, a new nation of sixty-four million people, had been asserting its power since the accession of the young Kaiser, Wilhelm II. Wilhelm had dismissed the brilliant Otto von Bismarck in 1890 and took foreign policy matters into his own hands. Believing that Germany should "have a place in the sun" (meaning a share of the glory and land that was being claimed by European countries throughout the world in a new age of imperialism), the Kaiser knocked heads with the British, the French, the Italians, the Chinese, and the Moroccans—and the list goes on from there. Though Germany finally achieved the overseas empire that the Kaiser and many Germans desired, these territories in Africa and Asia cost the Germans more than they profited from them.

Bismarck believed that Germany had grown to its natural size and that any attempt to expand it beyond its boundaries of 1871 was a mistake that would likely provoke a hostile response. The creation of Germany came at the expense of France, which had been humiliated in the Franco-Prussian War of 1870–71. France had been the most populous and richest nation on the European continent, but virtually overnight, it was supplanted by Germany. France had also lost the provinces of Alsace and Lorraine to Germany but vowed to get them back. France, along with Britain and Russia, began a process of rearmament after 1871 that put it on a collision course. Naturally, Germany did the same, and after things had been ironed out with Austria, the empire joined Germany in a defense pact and armed itself heavily as well. The stage was set for World War I.

You'll notice that Denmark and the valuable territory of Norway were not mentioned in the paragraph above. Neither were the Netherlands nor Belgium. Although these nations were valuable in their own ways (the Netherlands was, as it is now, one of the wealthiest European nations), they were not perceived as military threats to any of the Great Powers mentioned above. All of them, despite having leanings toward one nation or another, wished to stay out of any conflicts. Denmark and the Netherlands both declared neutrality. Belgium was aligned with France and Britain, though it maintained fairly good relations with Germany. It had to; Belgium and Germany shared a border. In 1910, Belgium's population was just under 7.5 million. Denmark's population was just over two and a half million, and Denmark did not share a border with France to help back it up.

Denmark is surrounded on three sides by water, so the Danes also had to take into account the actions of the British Royal Navy. Relations with Great Britain in 1914 were good, but the Danes knew from bitter experience that the British would not allow control of Denmark to fall to the Germans. This would increase the area from which the growing German Navy (*Kriegsmarine*) could operate would give them control of not only Denmark's excellent harbors and shipbuilding sites but also its powerful coastal fortresses. There was also the possibility that if the Germans conquered Denmark or secured passage of its troops through the country, the resource-rich nation of Sweden would be an easy conquest, as it was just a mile or two away across the straits.

For Germany's part, it wanted to prevent British control of Danish ports. If Britain gained control, they would have a closer base of operations from which to move against German ports on the North

Sea. This would make it vastly easier for the British to attack German ports on the Baltic (Kiel, Germany's naval base, is on the Baltic Sea). The Germans let the Danes know, in no uncertain terms, that should Denmark allow the British access through its waters into the Baltic, Germany would seize control of the country and its ports. The phrase "between a rock and a hard place" could not be more apt.

Between 1902 and 1910, the Danes looked for a way to protect themselves. The Danish Defense Commission was formed in 1902 to examine the situation from every angle and make recommendations regarding Denmark's future military choices. Denmark's "defense" consisted, for the most part, of its coastal defenses, which allowed it to play an outsized role in the region since it controlled sea traffic. However, since 1864, the Danes had made the conscious decision to limit their defense spending to only cover what was deemed necessary to dissuade a potential enemy. They did not seek to create a military that would pose a threat to anyone or be able to prevent a determined invasion from the south (and there was only one country on its southern border: Germany). In the end, the Danes had to choose which threat to address, and the more immediate threat to their country was Wilhelm's Germany.

In the few years before the war, the Danes entered into detailed negotiations with the Germans to try to hammer out an agreement that would guarantee the Danes a modicum of security while allaying German fears of British occupation. There was no formal result to the talks, but the British knew of them and created their own policy to deal with Denmark should war break out, which it did in August 1914.

Denmark was involved almost immediately. The Germans gave the Danes an ultimatum: they could either mine the entrances to the Baltic to block the British (and give Germany the maps detailing the mines' location), or the German Navy would do it on its own. This means the Danes would not know where the mines were, curtailing their trade with Sweden, Finland, and other countries to the east, namely Russia.

Danish King Christian X was a known friend of the British, and even he thought it was best to mine the Baltic approaches. The prime minister, along with the defense and foreign affairs ministries, were unsure of what position to take, so they let the king take the lead. What they did not know was the king had arranged for the mines to be laid but not armed. This was shortly relayed to the British, who remained skeptical, especially when a fishing boat exploded after hitting one of the "disarmed" mines. The question of mining the straits did not, in the end, have any great effect on Denmark's position during the war, but it does illustrate the desperately tight jam that the country was in.

The Danes enjoyed the diplomatic expertise of Foreign Minister Erik Scavenius from the beginning of the war until 1920. Scavenius managed to walk the tightrope between Germany and Britain and somehow managed both sides to allow Danish trade to flow to both the Allies (Britain and France) and Germany. Scavenius convinced both sides that it was in their best interest to allow Denmark to trade freely. The British, who at times during the early part of the war were desperately short on food, received Danish food exports, mostly ham, cheese, and butter. The Germans were able to access Denmark's resources, and Denmark also served as a conduit for Swedish and Norwegian goods to be sold in Germany.

Illustration 20: A picture of Erik Scavenius.
https://commons.wikimedia.org/wiki/File:Erik_Scavenius_1_(cropped).jpg

Due to Denmark's position between the two sides, it was uniquely qualified to broker peace between them. Throughout most of the war, Scavenius, King Christian X, and Prime Minister Thorvald Stauning (the leader of the powerful and increasingly influential Social Democratic Party of Denmark) made overtures to both the British and Germans. But since each side believed at different times that "victory was just around the corner," neither of them had much incentive to make a peace that would likely be costly in some manner and anger significant portions of their respective populations. It was hard to agree on peace when millions of soldiers had sacrificed their lives for victory—whatever that might look like.

Toward the end of the war, the Danes were increasingly fearful that Britain might move to occupy Denmark as a way to end the trench warfare on the Western Front, which would likely result in the Germans moving troops into the country. That would make Denmark perhaps the last battlefield of the world's deadliest conflict, at least at that point in history.

The Danes entered into talks with their southern neighbors about the possibility of German troops entering Denmark. These talks were headed by Erik Scavenius, who tempted the Germans with the hope that they might be able to control access to the Baltic themselves, as well as access to all of Denmark's export goods. Scavenius deliberately drew these talks out and pretended to need "further consultation" with the government and the Danish king every time the Germans pushed him to sign an agreement. Scavenius had connections in the British government, as did King Christian X, who was British King George V's cousin (one the British king liked, as opposed to one of his other cousins, Kaiser Wilhelm II, whom he did not like at all). The British kept them apprised of much of British policy throughout the war.

By the time Germany began to unravel with the entry of the United States in 1917 and the failure of its 1918 Spring Offensive, the Germans had put the Danish question on the back burner. Every man was needed at the front, not in Denmark. When the war ended in November 1918, the Danes had managed to stay out of the conflict and had limited its losses to a relatively small number of ships that either struck mines or were accidentally fired upon by one side or the other.

During WWI, Denmark was able to concentrate much of its energy on continued reforms, something that many of the war's belligerents could not. The changes that took place were revolutionary and would lay more of the groundwork for the modern Danish state that emerged after WWII.

In 1915, the Danes wrote a new constitution, appropriately known as the 1915 Constitution. Though most of it was similar to the Constitution of 1864, a few advanced laws were amended, including a law that said there were to be two houses of parliament, giving women the vote, establishing health insurance and safety protocols for industrial workers, and the breaking up of some of the remaining large landholdings, which were then redistributed more equitably. One must remember that Denmark is smaller than the US state of West Virginia, and the population was (and still is) large for its size. With so many large estates, much of the population did not have a chance to own land. What's more, not all of those estates were farms, so breaking them up for farmland increased Danish productivity in a significant way.

Lastly, the parliament began to use taxation to not only raise revenue but also steer Danes toward widely shared goals or beliefs. During WWI, alcohol taxes were increased, but food subsidies were given with the money. After the war and to the present day, Danish lawmakers, with the input of constituents, have continued this policy. Today, the biggest example is the tremendous tax on cars that burn gas or diesel. This is a response to the environmental crisis, but it also discourages the almost-continuous traffic jams found in many urban areas of western Europe and the US. Part of the tax on these vehicles goes directly to fund renewable energy in the country, particularly wind power.

Though the Danes did not share in the physical devastation of WWI or have to rebuild their economies, the Danes did suffer from the economic consequences of the war and the Great Depression.

Aside from the collapse of the worldwide economy in 1929, the economy of Denmark suffered due to the conflicts between the political parties in the country, which were thankfully non-violent. For virtually all of the 20th century, Danish politics was dominated by the same four parties: the Liberals, Conservatives, Social Democrats, and Radicals.

The Liberals were liberal in the sense that they followed the principles of 19th-century political thought: free speech, free press, removing hereditary power, and limiting the power of the landed elites.

The Conservatives, generally speaking, believed in a free-market system with very little control by the government. They wanted a hard limit to the reforms that resulted in expensive insurance and welfare schemes, which were brought about by the dominant Social Democrats and Radicals. The Conservatives were also in favor of a stronger monarchy and opposed most moves to increase the power of parliament and the lower classes.

The Social Democrats believed in the equitable sharing of power and land. They were willing to put these policies into law when they were in power, which was opposed by the Conservatives and some Liberals. Some of the rhetoric of the Social Democrats, who were in power from 1930 until 1940, alarmed many in Denmark. At times, they sounded like statements coming from Joseph Stalin's Soviet Union, which was the enemy of capitalists, conservatives, and others at the time. The Social Democrats came under much criticism for some of their statements; for instance, their leader, Thorvald Stauning, once said that his party wanted to "reform society and then control it," which sounds quite ominous. Stauning was forced to make his intentions clear. Although there was still opposition from Conservatives throughout Denmark, in the end, the policy that emerged was not that of a communist takeover of the industry but shared and collective ownership, along with shared responsibilities. The creation of a large "social safety net" is still the hallmark of Danish society and politics today.

The Radical Party (today's Danish Social Liberal Party) was not as radical as its name might suggest (at least not in today's terms). They surely were not Stalinists, as many wanted to believe at the time. Though they did share some ideas with more leftist parties in other nations, such as France, they were never as radical. The Radicals believed many of the same things as the Social Democrats, but they also hoped to change the culture of the country to bring it in line with their beliefs (equality for all, women's rights, criminal reform, educational reform, and free access). They spurred on the Social Democrats, with whom they often collaborated.

Denmark suffered from incredible inflation during the early 1920s, much like its German neighbor. Part of this was to pay for subsidies and support for farms (there was a near famine in Denmark for a period in the 1920s) and industries suffering from the worldwide economic depression. Unlike many other nations at the time, the Danes managed to come out of the worst of the Great Depression by the early 1930s by reforming the monetary system. Trade began to slowly increase as the decade went on.

By 1940, Denmark was a relatively stable country. It enjoyed an economic rejuvenation and was generally free from the political strife that the rest of Europe felt. There was only one real concern: what would Adolf Hitler, who gained power in 1933, do?

The Danish Nazi Party (The National Socialist Workers' Party of Denmark or *Danmarks Nationalsocialistiske Arbejderparti*, the "DNSAP") was not popular in the years before WWII, but during the war, the DNSAP acted as an auxiliary and secret police role at the behest of the Gestapo (Hitler's secret police).

WWII began on September 1st, 1939, with Germany's invasion of Poland. On September 3rd, Britain and France declared war on Hitler, fulfilling a promise made to Poland. For nine months after the invasion of Poland, the world waited to see what would happen in the spring. On April 9th, 1940, the Danes would find out.

Chapter 13 – World War II

Denmark was fully aware of its position as Hitler's northern neighbor. With a population of about five million compared to Germany's seventy million and with an army barely the size of Berlin's police force, the Danes knew that any opposition to Hitler, should he decide to invade, was virtually useless. When the invasion did come on April 9th, 1940, some Danish units put up a resistance. They were brushed aside easily. Some fired a few bullets or shells toward the Germans for the sake of "honor," but most simply went home. Late in the afternoon of April 9th, the Danish government announced that it was surrendering to the Germans to prevent the destruction of its cities by air. The Danish Air Force was virtually nonexistent. Germany's air force (the *Luftwaffe*) very much existed and in great numbers.

Denmark is an unusual case in the history of WWII. Given its proximity to Germany, there was less open opposition to the Nazis than there was in Norway, for example, but unwritten rules of behavior toward the occupiers were followed by most Danes, except the relatively small (but growing) number of Danish Nazis. Women were not to "consort" with Germans. German commands were to be followed slowly. More than likely, many German soldiers and officers ingested a great deal of Danish saliva in their restaurant meals during the war.

Though life under Hitler's regime was not easy for anyone, comparatively speaking, it was for Denmark. The two nations had shared a border for an incredibly long time, much trade was done between the two, families were intertwined, and the ethnic similarities (both real and imagined by Hitler) were great. Hitler adopted a *relatively* benevolent attitude toward the Danes because of his racial worldview, which included the Danish people. This worldview, of course, was his nebulous fantasy idea of a group of people called the Aryans. To Hitler, the Scandinavians were the epitome of his "racially pure Germanic race." Their relative isolation had left them "unsullied" by intermarriage with "lesser" European peoples outside of Germany and Austria, the latter of which was Hitler's homeland. (As a side note, Hitler occupied Norway later that spring, while Sweden walked a fine line of neutrality.)

The Danes were allowed to run their own internal affairs as long as they fell into line with Nazi plans. Even Social Democrat Thorvald Stauning was allowed to remain prime minister, and he tried to walk a very fine line. King Christian X remained in the country, despite calls for him to go into exile. Christian played a very subtle game with the Nazi occupiers. He used coded language and symbols of resistance to show his opposition to the Nazis and the occupation. For most, he became an inspiration, though stories of him wearing a Star of David in support of Denmark's Jews are apocryphal (as is the legend of Copenhagen's Danish citizens doing the same).

Illustration 21: Christian X on his daily, unguarded ride through Copenhagen, surrounded by adoring citizens. This continued virtually uninterrupted until the war's end. Christian (d. 1947) was one of the most popular kings in Danish history.
https://commons.wikimedia.org/wiki/File:Christian_X_of_Denmark_on_horse_at_Gyldenl%C3%B8vesgade.jpg

Despite the preferred treatment received by the Danes, they were still required to fill a certain number of Waffen SS (the military branch of Hitler's dreaded organization). A battalion-sized Danish Legion was formed, and a certain number of Danes volunteered for the all-Scandinavian Waffen-SS division (the 5th SS "Wiking"), but this number was never near the total that Hitler had hoped for.

Of course, like every other nation occupied by the Nazis, the Danes were subjected to Hitler's oppressive laws against Jews. Danish Jews were to be deported to the extermination camps being planned and erected in Poland.

Though anti-Semitism did have adherents in Denmark, the level of this was quite less than in other German-occupied territories, especially in eastern Europe. The Danish Nazis, the SS, and the Gestapo were responsible for rounding Jews up in September 1943. The following account is one of the bright stars in the incredibly dark sky covering Europe from 1939 to 1945.

The German command received orders to "evacuate" the Jews of Denmark, which included a number of German Jews who had fled before the war. The estimated Jewish population before the war was approximately 7,500, with 1,500 being German Jewish refugees. Most but not all of Denmark's Jews lived in Copenhagen or its suburbs.

In Denmark, the German commander, Georg Duckwitz, knew what "evacuation" for the Jews meant. Most Germans in high places did, and if they did not know the exact final result, they knew that, at the very least, "evacuation" meant great suffering. Duckwitz flew to Berlin and asked for clarification of his orders and for them to be rescinded; of course, he was rebuffed. He then secretly flew to Stockholm, Sweden, consulted with Swedish Prime Minister Per Hansson, and asked the Swede if his government would give the Jews a safe place if they could manage to cross the narrow straits to his country.

Hansson's answer was yes, and Duckwitz returned to Denmark. Through back channels and informants, he was able to make contact with the Danish resistance movement. Over the course of the next two weeks, Danish fishing vessels hid their Jewish brothers in their holds and smuggled them to Sweden, where they remained in safety throughout the war. Seven thousand Jews managed to make the dangerous trip. A few lost their lives when a few boats were fired upon, but less than five hundred Danish Jews were rounded up during the war. Most of these were sent to the so-called "Artist's Camp" of Theresienstadt in Czechoslovakia, where most survived due to pressure from the Danish Red Cross. Though the numbers could have been much worse, it should be remembered that some 120 to 130 Danish Jews died in the Holocaust.

As the years of occupation continued, more and more Danes rose up or took part in resistance movements throughout the country. As the war went on, the Germans requisitioned more Danish food and other goods. Shortages began to be felt, and the people began to go hungry. The Danish police, which was virtually all Nazis (though some were plants by the Danish Resistance), were brutal in their pursuit of resisters and were at times more rabid than the Nazis themselves in their methods. This caused more resistance, as did reports of both German atrocities throughout Europe and the turning of the tide against Hitler. By 1943, the Danes had managed to sabotage hundreds of German facilities or industries that contributed to the war effort, and the Nazis cracked down.

This crackdown led to widespread strikes, which led to more arrests, torture, and even more strikes. In the first part of the war, there were many Danish resistance groups, most of whom worked without coordinating plans, which sometimes led to bungled operations and arrests. In September 1943, the Danish Freedom Council was created to unify and coordinate the different groups. Eventually, some twenty thousand Danes (men, women, and children) joined the resistance movements, and many more aided them covertly.

One of the more famous resistance movements in Denmark was known as Holger Danske, named after a famous Middle Age hero who would be reborn in Denmark's hour of greatest need. One of the many functions of Holger Danske and other groups, especially in Danish cities, was the intimidation and occasional assassination of Danish collaborators. Toward the end of the war, many Danish police officers and other figures had seen the "writing on the wall" as far as Germany's defeat went and changed sides. Others were scared of possible retribution after the war was over, and they supplied the resistance movements with insider information about German plans. The amount of information increased after D-Day, which was the invasion of Normandy by the Western Allies in June 1944.

The months and weeks before D-Day saw the Danish Resistance spring into mass action in coordination with the British secret operations unit, the SOE (Special Operations Executive). So many instances of resistance and sabotage took place that the Germans were not able to send troops from Denmark to France to help repel the

Allies. This caused the Germans to take direct control of policing the country, and in the last months of the war, sabotages, assassinations, arrests, and executions went up. Street battles were fought in Copenhagen toward the war's end. One of the more tragic episodes of the war was the bombing of "Shell House" (Shellhus), the police headquarters in Copenhagen where the Gestapo kept those suspected of being in the Resistance. The Resistance believed the Germans were about to get information that would result in the destruction of the movement, so the decision was made to bomb Shell House. It was hoped that a number of those in the Resistance would be able to escape, but if not, their deaths would prevent important information from being divulged. The result of the bombing was tragic. Though eighteen Danish resistance fighters were able to escape, the inexact nature of bombing at the time meant that there were many civilian casualties (of the 125 Danes killed, 86 were children). Eight prisoners had also died; they had been "housed" within the roof beams as human shields to prevent this type of attack from happening. The building was all but destroyed, and forty-five collaborators were killed, as well as fifty-five Germans.

Denmark and Norway were both liberated largely by themselves, though the Nazis had begun to flee to Germany before the end actually came. Before the war ended, the Western Allies made Denmark a priority, even over Berlin. Control of Denmark by the powerful Allied navies and a large number of British troops in the country meant that the Soviet Union, which was driving hard to obtain Denmark, could not expand its influence to the tiny but important nation.

(For more on Holger Danske and the bombing of Shell House, watch *Flame & Citron* and Flame" (currently on Amazon Prime Video) and *The Bombardment* on Netflix.)

Conclusion

After WWII, Denmark was quick to protect itself from the growing power of the Soviet Union and joined NATO (North Atlantic Treaty Organization) as one of its original members in 1949. While passing the Danish straits is "toll-free" today, Denmark and Norway, which is also a NATO member, would be called upon to close sea traffic to Russia in the event of war. Though the Royal Danish Army is small, it is highly trained and has taken part in peace-keeping missions and combat duty in Afghanistan. The Royal Danish Navy is regarded as a small but highly effective force. The Royal Danish Air Force, which is soon to be equipped with a number of the most advanced American fighters, is Denmark's largest and most effective military branch.

After the war, the Danish social welfare state as we know it today was refined and added to. The most noticeable element of this social safety net is universal free healthcare. Since the advent of universal healthcare, the rate of most major diseases caused by lifestyle is much less in Denmark than in other Western countries outside Scandinavia. Cigarettes and alcohol are highly taxed, as are some types of food, especially those with excess sugar.

Women's rights were expanded in the 1950s and 1960s, and laws protecting women's careers due to pregnancy were passed. More jobs had been opened to women to the point where there is almost gender parity in most workplaces today. Abortion was legalized in 1973. In the late 1990s and into the 21st century, Danish men began taking a significant role in parenting. Paid paternal leave and maternal leave have allowed parents to retain their role in the workplace and have improved the quality of child-rearing in the country. Guaranteed universal daycare also helps. Seventy-five to eighty percent of Danish women between sixteen and sixty-six have jobs.

Denmark was one of the first nations to recognize the rights of people of different sexual orientations; it did so in 1933, though discrimination based on sexual preference continued for some time. Same-sex marriage was allowed in the late 1980s, but same-sex marriage in the Danish church was not allowed until 2012. In 2010, same-sex couples were given the right to adopt.

Today, Denmark is one of the freest nations in terms of sexual preference, with legal protections enshrined in its constitution. It has also recognized transgender people. Danish transgender people were protected by the law when the possibility of gender reassignment surgery became a reality in the late 1970s, but they were forced to become sterilized and had to receive medical approval. The sterilization element was removed some time ago, and in 2014, transgender people were able to get gender reassignment surgery without medical approval.

Today, Denmark spends about 50 percent of its tax revenue on public expenditures, like medical insurance and education. This does mean that its tax rate is one of the highest in the world (it is behind Sweden), but in recent years, it has come down. However, most Danes support higher taxes for the efficient administration of these social programs.

So, we end where we began. For all of the reasons mentioned in this book, especially in the last chapters, Denmark has enjoyed being the "happiest nation on Earth" a number of times. And when it hasn't been declared *the* happiest, it's always in the top five, usually in the top three, along with other Scandinavian countries, such as Finland.

Here's another book by Captivating History that you might like

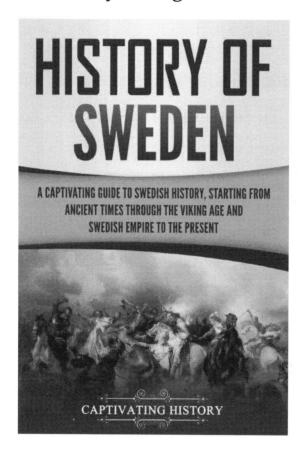

Free Bonus from Captivating History (Available for a Limited time)

Hi History Lovers!

Now you have a chance to join our exclusive history list so you can get your first history ebook for free as well as discounts and a potential to get more history books for free! Simply visit the link below to join.

Captivatinghistory.com/ebook

Also, make sure to follow us on Facebook, Twitter and Youtube by searching for Captivating History.

Bibliography

"Ancient Roman Artifact Found on Danish Island." ScienceNordic. Last modified April 22, 2015. https://sciencenordic.com/archaeology-cultural-history-denmark/ancient-roman-artifact-found-on-danish-island/1416970

"A Brief History of LGBTQI+ Rights in Denmark." Scandinavia Standard. Last modified August 8, 2017. https://www.scandinaviastandard.com/a-brief-history-of-lgbtqi-rights-in-denmark

Captivating History. FRENCH HISTORY: A CAPTIVATING GUIDE TO THE HISTORY OF FRANCE, CHARLEMAGNE, AND NOTRE-DAME DE PARIS. Captivating History, 2021.

"Christianity Comes to Denmark." National Museum of Denmark. Accessed March 14, 2022. https://en.natmus.dk/historical-knowledge/denmark/prehistoric-period-until-1050-ad/the-viking-age/religion-magic-death-and-rituals/christianity-comes-to-denmark/

"The Danish Jewish Museum - 400 Years of Danish Jewish History." Accessed April 12, 2022. https://jewmus.dk/en/the-danish-jewish-museum/

"DNA Reveals Details of Scandinavian Battle Axe Culture." Life in Norway. Last modified April 20, 2021.

https://www.lifeinnorway.net/dna-reveals-details-of-scandinavian-battle-axe-culture/

Ed. "'To Be or Not to Be': Hamlet's Soliloquy with Analysis." No Sweat Shakespeare. Last modified January 26, 2021. https://nosweatshakespeare.com/quotes/soliloquies/to-be-or-not-to-be/

"How a Heinous Act of Genocide Doomed Aethelred the Unready's Kingdom." History Hit. Accessed March 11, 2022. https://www.historyhit.com/1002-attempted-genocide-englands-danes/

"How Accurate Are the Viking Sagas?" TheCollector. Last modified February 1, 2022. https://www.thecollector.com/viking-sagas-historical-mythology

Kessler, P. L. "Kingdoms of Northern Europe - Jutes (Eudoses)." The History Files. Accessed March 9, 2022. https://www.historyfiles.co.uk/KingsListsEurope/ScandinaviaJutes.htm

"King Frederik II of Denmark and Norway and Duke of Schleswig – European Royal History." European Royal History. Accessed April 3, 2022. https://europeanroyalhistory.wordpress.com/tag/king-frederik-ii-of-denmark-and-norway-and-duke-of-schleswig

"Prosperous Vikings Whitewashed Their Walls." ScienceNordic. Last modified October 13, 2013. https://sciencenordic.com/archaeoloy-chemistry-denmark/prosperous-vikings-whitewashed-their-walls/1391621

UN/Sustainable Development Solutions Network. Accessed February 15, 2022. https://worldhappiness.report/